PURANAS

PURANAS

OR

AN ACCOUNT OF THEIR CONTENTS AND NATURED

BY

H. H. WILSON

GYAN

Published by

Gyan Publishing House
5, Ansari Road
Daryaganj, New Delhi-110002
Phone: 011-47034999, 9811692060
E-mail: books@gyanbooks.com

Distribution Network
gyanbooks.com
India, USA, Canada, UK, Australia

ISBN: 978-81-212-7017-5 (PB)
First Published, 1897

2nd Impression 2024

Printed at: Gyan Press, Delhi.

PURANAS
Author: H. H. WILSON

PURANAS

OR

(AN ACCOUNT OF THEIR CONTENTS AND NATURE)

BY

H. H. WILSON.

PREFACE.

——:o:——

The following pages, from the pen of Professor Wilson whose name India will never forget, from the introduction to his translation of the Vishnu Purana. They are so well written, with a complete and excellent synopsis of all the Puranas that a reprint of them with occasional changes, we are sure, will serve the purpose of this treatise. The literature, passing by the name of Puranas, is so very voluminous that it is not possible for one man to go through them during his life time. This sketch however will give them an idea of what all the Puranas contain—their nature and the probable date of composition. As it is not possible to ascertain accurately the date of various compositions we have not entered into details on this subject and have contented ourselves with merely placing before our readers the view of the learned author.

The sketch, as it is, is quite sufficient for a general reader to have an idea of the contents of the Puranas; those, who wish to learn more, should either resort to the original works or their translations.

CALCUTTA,
June 1897.

CONTENTS.

PURANAS.

THEOLOGY & ANTIQUITY.

THE literature of the Hindus has now been cultivated, for many years, with singular diligence, and, in many of its branches, with eminent success. There are some departments, however, which are yet but partially and imperfectly investigated; and we are far from being in possession of that knowledge which the authentic writings of the Hindus alone can give us of their best religion, mythology and historical traditions.

From the materials to which we have hitherto had access, it seems probable that there have been three principal forms in which the religion of the Hindus has existed, at as many different periods. The duration of those periods, the circumstances of their succession, and the precise state of the national faith at each season, it is not possible to trace with any approach to accuracy. The premises have been too imperfectly determined to authorize other than conclusions of a general and somewhat vague description; and those remain to be hereafter confirmed, or corrected, by more extensive and satisfactory researches.

The earliest form under which the Hindu religion appears is that taught in the Vedas. The style of the language, and the purport of the composition, of those works, as far as we are acquainted with them, indicate a date long anterior to that of any other class of Sanskrit writings. It is yet, however, scarcely safe to advance an opinion of the precise belief, or philosophy which they inculcate. To enable us to judge of their tendency, we have only a general sketch of their arrangement and contents, with a few extracts, by Mr. Colebrooke, in the Asiatic researches; a few incidental observations by Mr. Ellis, in the same miscellany; and a translation of the first book of the Sanhita, or collection of the prayers of Rig-Veda, by Dr. Rosen; and some of the Upanishads, or speculative treatises, attached to, rather than part of, the Vedas, by Rammohun Roy. Of the religion taught in the Vedas, Mr.

Colebrooke's opinion will probably be received as that which is best entitled to deference; as, certainly, no Sanskrit scholar has been equally conversant with the original works. The real doctrine of the whole Indian scripture is the unity of the Deity, in whom the universe is comprehended; and the seeming polytheism, which it exhibits, offers the elements, and the stars and planets, as gods. The three principle manifestations of the divinity, with other personified attributes and energies, and most of the other gods of Hindu mythology, are indeed mentioned, or, at least indicated, in the Vedas. But the worship of deified heroes is no part of that system; nor are the incarnations of deities suggested in any other portion of the text I have yet seen; though such are sometimes hinted by the commentators. Some of these statements may, perhaps, require modification; for without a careful examination of all the prayers of the Vedas, it would be hazardous to assert that they contain one indication whatever of hero-worship; and, certainly, they do appear to allude, occasionally, to the Avataras or incarnations of Vishnu. Still, however, it is true that the prevailing character of the ritual of the Vedas is the worship of the personified elements; of Agni or fire; Indra, the firmanent;

Vayu, the air; Varuna, the water; of Aditya, the sun; Soma the moon; and other elementary and planetary personages. It is also true that worship of the Vedas is, for the most part domestic worship consisting of prayers and oblations offered in their own houses, not in temples, by individuals, for individual good, and addressed to unreal presence not to visible types. In a word, the religion of the Vedas was not idolatry.

It is not possible to conjecture when its simple and primititive form of adoration was succeeded by the worship of images and types, representing Brahma, Vishnu, Siva, and other imaginary beings, consisting of a mythological pantheon of most ample extent; or when Rama and Krishna, who appear to have been, or originally, real and historical characters, were elevated to the dignity of divinities. Image-worship is alluded to by Manu, in several passages, but with an intimation that those Brahmanas who subsist by ministering in temples are an inferior and degraded class. The story of Rámàyan and Mahabharata turns wholly upon the doctrine of incarnation; all the chief dramatis personœ of the poems being impersonations of gods, and demi-gods and celestial spirits. The ritual appears to be that of the Vedas; and it may be doubted if any allusion to image-worship occurs. But the doctrine of propitiation by penance and praise prevails throughout; and Vishnu and Siva are the especial objects of penegyric and invocation. In these two works, then, we trace unequivocal indications of departure from the elemental worship of the Vedas, and the origin or elaboration of legends which form the great body of the mythological religion of the Hindus. How far they only improved upon the cosmogony and chronology of their predecessors, or in what degree the traditions of families and dynaties originated with them, are questions that can only be determined when the Vedas and the two works in question shall have been more thoroughly examined. The different works known by the name of Puranas are evidently derived from the same religious system as the Ramayana and Mahabharata or from the mythologic stage of the Hindu belief They present, however, pecularities which designate their belonging to a later period, and to an important modication in the progress of opinion. They repeat the theoretical cosmogony of the two great poems; they expand and systematize the chronological computation; and they give a more definite and connected representation of the mythological fictions and the historical traditions. But besides these and other particulars which may be derivable from an old, if not from a primitive era, 'they offer characteristic pecularities of a more modern description, In the paramount importance which they assign to individual divinities in the variety and purport of the rites and observances addressed to them, and in the invention of new legends illustrative of the power and graciousness of those deities and of the efficacy of implicit devotion to them. Siva and Vishnu under one or other form are almost the sole objects that claim the homage of the Hindus, in the Puranas; departing from the domestic and elemental ritual of the Vedas, and exhibiting a sectarial fervour and exclusiveness not traceable in the Ramayana and only to a qualified extent in the Mahabharata. They are no longer authorities for Hindu belief as a whole; 'they are special guides for separate and sometimes, conflicting branches of it; compiled for the evident purpose of promoting the preferential, or in some cases, the sole worship of Vishnu or of Shiva.

That the Puranas always bore the character here given of them may admit of reasonable doubt; that it correctly applies to them as they are now met with, the following pages will clearly substantiate. It is possible however, that there may have been an earlier class of Puranas of which those we now have, are but the partial and adulterated representatives. The identity of the legends in many of them, and still more the identity of the words—for, in several of them, long passages are literally the same—is a sufficient proof that, in all such cases they must be copied either from some other similar work, or from a common and prior original. It is not unsual, also for a fact to be stated upon the authority of an old stanza, which is cited accordingly; showing the existence of an earlier source of information: and, in very many instances, legends are alluded to, not told; evincing acquaintance with their prior narration some where else. The name itself Purana, which implies 'old,' indicates the object of the compilation to be the preservation of ancient traditions; a purpose, in the present condition of the Puranas, very imperfectly fulfilled. Whatever weight may be attached to these considerations, there is no disputing evidence to the like effect, afforded by other and unquestionable authority. The description given by Mr. Colebrook, of the contents of a Purana is taken from Sanskrit writers. The Lexicon of Amara Sinha gives, as a synonym of Purana, Panchalakshna, that which has five characteristic topics; and there is no difference of opinion, among the scholars, as to what these are.

They are, as Mr. Colebrooke mentions: I, Primary creation or cosmogony; II, Secondary creation, or the destruction and renovation of worlds, including chronology; III. Genealogy of gods and patriarchs; IV. Reigns of Manus, or periods called Manwantaras; and V. History, or such particulars as have been preserved of the princes of the solar and lunar races, and of their descendants in modern times. Such, at any rate, were the constituent and characteristic portions of a Purana, in the days of Amara Sinha, fifty-six years before the Christian era; and, if the Puranas had undergone no change since his time, such we should expect to find them still. Do they conform to this description? Not exactly, in any one instance; to some of them it is ntterly applicable; to others it only partially applies. There is not one to which it belongs so entirely as to the Vishnu Purana; and it is one of the circumstances which gives to this work a more authentic character than most of its fellows can pretend to. Yet, even in this instance, we have a book upon the institutes of society and obsequial rites interposed between Manwantaras and the genealogies of princes; and a life of Krishna separating the latter from an account of the end of the world; besides the insertion of various legends of a manifestly popular and sectarial character. No doubt, many of the Puranas as they now are, correspond with the view which Colonel Vans Kennedy takes of their purport. "I cannot discover, in them," he remarks, "any other object than that of religious instruction." The description of the earth and of the planetary system, and the lists of Royal races that occur in them," he asserts to be evidently extraneous, and not essential circumsiances; as they are omitted in some Puranas and very concisely illustrated in others; while on the contrary, in all the Puranas, some or other of the leading principles, rites and observances of the Hindu religion are fully dwelt upon and illustrated either by suitable legends or by prescribing the ceremonies to be practised, and the prayers and invocations to be employed, in the worship of different deities." Now, however accurate this description may be of the Puranas as they are, it is clear that it does not apply to what they were when they were synonymously designated as Panch-lakshanas or 'treatise on five topics,' not one of which five is ever specified by text of comment, to be religious instruction. In the knowledge of Amara Singha the lists of princes were not extraneous and unessential; and their being now so considered by a writer so well acqainted with the contents of

Puranas as Colonel Van Kennedy, is a decisive proof that, since the days of the lexicographer they have undergone some material alteration, and that we have not, at present, the same works, in all res-respects, that were current, under the denomination of Puranas, in the century prior to Christianity.

The inference deduced from the discrepancy between the actual form and the older definition of Purana, unfavourable to the antiquity of the extant works generally, is converted into certainty when we come to examine them in detail. For although they have no dates attached to them circumstances are sometimes mentioned, or attached to, or references to authority are made, or legends are narrated, or places are particularised, of which the comparatively recent date is indisputable, and which enforce a corresponding reduction of the antiquity of the work in which they are discovered; at the same time, they may be acquitted of subservience to any but sectarial imposture. They were pious frauds for temporary purposes: they never emanated from any impossible combination of the Brahmanas to fabricate for the antiquity of the entire Hindu system any claims which it cannot fully support. A very great portion, of the contents of all, is genuine and old. The sectarial interpolation or embellishment is always sufficiently palpable to be set aside without injury to the more authentic and primitive material; and the Puranas, although they belong especially to that stage of the Hindu religion in which faith in some one divinity was the prevailing principle, are, also a valuable record of the form of Hindu belief which came next in order to that of the Vedas, which grafted hero-worship upon the simpler ritual of the latter; and which had been adopted, and was extensively, perhaps universally, established in India, at the time of the Greek invasion. The Hercules of the Greek writer was, indubitably, the Balarama of the Hindus; and their notices of Muthura on the Jamuna and of the kingdom of the Suraseni and the Pandya country, evidence the prior currency of the traditions which constitute the argumeut of the Mahabharata and which are constantly repeated in the Puranas, relating to the Pandava and Yadava races to Krishna and his contemporary heroes, and to the dynasties of the solar and lunar kings.

The theogony and cosmogonv of the Puranas may, probably, be traced to the Vedas. They are not, as far as is yet known, described in detail in those works; but they are frequently alluded to ,in a train more or less mystical and obscnre, which indicates acquaintance with their existence, and which seems to have supplied the Puranas with the groundwork of their systems. The scheme of primary or elementary creation they borrow from the Sankhya philosophy, which is probably, one of the oldest forms of speculation on men and nature, amongst the Hindus. Agreeably however, to that part of Pauranik character which there is reason to suspect of a later origin, their inculcation of the worship of a favourite deity, they combine the interposition of a creator with the independent evolution of matter, in a somewhat contradictory and in unintelligible style. It is evident, too that their account of secondary creation, or the development of the existing forms and things, and the disposition of the universe are derived from several and different sources; and it appears very likely that they are to be accused of some of the incongruities and absurdities by which the narrative is disfigured, in consequence of having attempted to assign reality and significancy to what was merely a metaphor or mysticism. There is however, amidst the unnecessary complexity of the discription, a general agreement amongst them as to the origin of things and their final distribution, and in many of the circumstances there is a striking concurrence with the ideas which seem to have prevaded the whole of the ancient world, and which ws, therefore, believe to be faithfully represented in the Puranas.

The pantheism of the Puranas is one of their invariable characteristics; although [the particular divinity who is all things, from whom all things proceed, and to whom all things return, be diversified according to their individual sectarial bias. They seem to have derived the notion from the Vedas; but, in them, the one universal Being is of a higher order than a personification of attributes or elements, and, however, imperfectly conceived or unworthily described, He is God. In the Puranas, the one only supreme Being is supposed to be manifest in the person of Shiva or Vishnu, either in the way of illusion, or in sport; and one or other of these divinities is, therefore also the cause of all that is,—is, himself, all that exists. The identity of God and nature is not a new notion: it was very general in the speculations of antiquity; but it assumed a new vigour in the early ages of Christianity, and was carried to an equal pitch of extravanance by the Platonic Christians as by the Saiva or Vaishnava Hindus. It seems not impossible that there was some communication betweem them. We know that there was an active communication between India and Red sea, in the early ages of the Christian era, and that doctrines, as well as articles of merchandise, were brought to Alexandria from the former,

Epiphanius and Eusebius accuse Scythians of having imported from India, in the second century, books on magic and hervtical notions leading to Manichæism; and it was at the same period that Ammonius Saccos instituted the sect of the new Platonists at Alexandria. The basis of the heresy was, that true philosophy derived its origin from the eastern nations. His doctrine of the identity of God and the universe is that of Vedas and Puranas; and the practices he enjoined, as well as their object, were precisely those described in several of the Puranas, under the name of God. His disciples were taught to extenuate, by mortification and contemplation, the bodily restraints upon the immortal spirit; so that, in this life, they might enjoy communion with the Supreme Being and ascend, after death, to the universal parent. That these are Hindu tenets, the following pages will testify; and, by the admission of their Alexandrian teacher, they originated in India. The importation was, perhaps, not wholly unrequitted: the loan may not have been unpaid. It is not impossible that the Hindu doctrines received fresh animation from their adoption by the successors of Ammonius, and, especially, by the mystics, who may have prompted, as well as employed, the expressions of Puranas.

Anquetil de Perron has given, in the introduction to his translation of the Oupnekhat, several hymns by Synesius, a bishop of the fifth century. which may eerve a parallel to many of the hymns and prayers addressed to Vishnu in the Vishnu Purana.

The ascription, to individual and personal deities, of the attributes of the one universal and and spiritual Supreme being, is an indication of a later date than the Vedas, certainly, and apparently also than the Ramayana, where Rama, although an incarnation of Vishnu, commonly appears in his human character alone. There is something of the kind in the Mahabharata, in respect to Krishna; especially in the philosophical episode known as the Bhagabad Gita. In other places the divine nature of Krishna is less decidedly affirmed; in some, it is disputed or denied; and in most of the situations in which he is exhibited in action, it is as a prince and warrior, not as a divinity. He exercises no superhuman faculties in the defence of himself or his friends, or in the defeat and destruction of his foes. The Mahabharata, however, is evidently, a work of various periods, and requires to be read throughout, carefully and critically, before its weight as an authority can be accurately appreciated. As it is now in type, thanks to the public spirit of the Asiatic Society of Bengal, and their secretary, Mr. J. Prinsep,—it will not be long before the Sanskrit scholars of thc continent will accurately appreciate its value.

The Puranas are, also, works of evidently different ages, and have been cempited under different circumstances, the precise nature of which we can but imperfectly conjecture from internal evidence. And from what we know of the history of religious opinion in India tt is highly probable that, of the present popular forms of the Hindu religion, none assumed their actual state earlier than the time of Sankara Acharya, the great Saiva reformer, who flourished, in the eighth or ninth century. Of the Vaishnava teachers Ramanuja dates in the twelfth century; Madhwacharja, in the thirteenth, and Vallabha, in the sixteenth; and the Puranas seemed to have accompanied or followed, their innovations, being obviously intended to advocate the doctrines they taught. This is to assign to some of them a very modern date, it is true: but I can not think that a higher can, with justice, be ascribed to them. This, however, applies to some only out of the number, as I shall presently proceed to specify.

Another evidence of a comparatively modern date must be admitted in those Chapters of the Puranas which, assuming a prophetic tone, foretell what dynasties of kings will reign in the Kali age. These Chapters, it is true, are found but in four of the Puranas; but they are conclusive in bringing down the date of those four to a period considerably subsequent to Christianity. It is also to be remarked that the Vayu, Vishnu, Bhagabata and Matsya Puranas in which these particulars are foretold, have, in all other respects, the character of as great antiquity as any works of their class. The invariave form of the Puranas is that of a dialogue, in which some person relates its contents, in reply to the inquiries of another. This dialogue is interwoven with others, which are repeated as having been held, on other occasions, between different individuals, in consequence of similar questions having been asked. The immediate narrator is, commonly, though not constantly, Lomaharshana or Romaharshana the disciciple of Vyasa, who is supposed to communicate what was imparted to him by his preceptor, as he had heard it from some other sage. Vyasa, as will be seen in the body of the work, is a generic title, meaning an 'arranger' or 'compiler.' It is, in this age, applied to Krishna Dwaipayan, the son of Parasara, who is said to have taught the Vedas and Puranas to various desciples, but who appears to have been the head of a college, or school, under whom various learned men gave to the sacred literature of the Hindus the form in which it now presents itself. In this task, the disciples, as they are termed, of Vyasa were, rather, his colleagues and coadjutors; for they were already conversant with what he is fabled to have taught them; and, amongst them, Lomaharshana represents the class of persons who were especially charged with the record of political and temporal events. He is called 'Suta,' as if it were a proper name, but is more correctly, a title; and Lomaharshana was 'a Suta,' that is a bard, or panegyrist, who was created according to our text, to celebrate the exploits of princes, and who according to the Vayu and Padma Puranas, has a right, by birth and profession, to narrate the Puranas, in preference even to Brahmanas. It is not unlikely, therefore, that we are to understand, by his being represented as the disciple of Vaysa, the institution of some attempt, made under the direction of the latter, to collect, from the heralds and annalists of his day, the scattered traditions which they had imperfectly preserved and hence the consequent appropriation of the Puranas, in a great measure, to the genealogies of regal dynasties and descriptions of the universe. However this may be, the machinary has been but loosely adhered to; and many of the Puranas, like the Vishnu, are refered to a different narrator.

An account is given, in Vishnu Purana of a series of Pauranic compilations of which in their present form, no vestige appears. Lomaharshana is said to have six disciples, three of whom composed as many fundamental Samhitas, whilst he himself completed a fourth. By a Samhita is generally understood a 'collection' or 'compilation.' The Samhita of Vedas are collections of hymns and prayers belonging to them, arranged according to the judgment of some individual sage, who is, therefore, looked upon as the originator and teacher of each. Tne Samhitas, of the Puranas, then should be analogous compilations, attributed, respectively to Maitreya, Samsapayana, Akritabrana, and Romaharshana; no such Puranic Samhitas are now known. The substance of the four is said to be collected in the Vishnu Purana, which is, also, in another place, itself called a Samhita. But such compilations have, not as far as inquiry has yet proceeded, been discovered. The specification may be accepted as an indication of Puranas' having existed in some other form, in which they are no longer met with; although it does not appear that the arrangement was incompatible with their existence as separate works; for the Vishnu Purana, which is our authority for the four Samhitas, gives us also, the usual enumeration of the several Puranas.

There is another classification of the Puranas alluded to in the Matsya Purana, and specified by the Padma Purana, but more fully. It is not undeserving of notice, as it expresses the opinion which native writers entertain of the scope of the Puranas, and of their recognizing the subservience of these works to the dissemination of sectarian principles. Thus, it is said, in the Uttar Kanda of the Padma, that the Puranas, as well as the other works are divided into three classes, according to the qualities which prevail in them. Thus the Vishnu, Naradiya, Bhagabata, Garuda, Padma, Baraha Puranas are Sattwika or pure, from the predominence, in them of the Sattwa quality, or that of goodness and purity. They are, in fact, Vaishnava Puranas. The Matsya, Kurma, Linga, Siva, Skanda, and Agni Puranas are Tamasa, or Puranas of darkness, from the prevalence of the quality of Tamas 'ignorance', 'gloom.' They are ·ndisputably Saiva Puranas. The third series comprising the Brahmanda, Brahma Vaivarta, Markandeya, Bhavishya, Vaman, and Brahma Puranas, are designated as Rajasa, 'passionate,' from Rajas, the property of passion, which they are supposed to represent. The Matsya does not specify which are the Puranas that come under these designations, but remarks that those in which the Mahatmya of Hari or Vishnu prevails, are Sattwika; those in which the legends of Agni or Siva predominate are Tamasa; and those which dwell most on the stories of Brahma are Rajas. I have elsewhere stated that I considered the Rajas Puranas to lean to the Sakta division of the Hindus, the worshippers of Sakti or the female principle; founding this opinion on the character of the legends which some of them contain, such as the Durga Mahatmya, or celebrated legend on which the worship of Durga or Kâli is especially fouuded which is a principal episode of the Markandeya. The Brahma Vaivarta also devotes the greatest portion of its chapter to the celebration to Radha, the mistress of Krishna. and other female divinities. Colonel Vans Kennedy however, objects to the application of the term. Sakta to this last division of the Puranas; the worship oi Sakti being the especial object of a different class of works, the Tantras; and not such form of worship being particularly incalculated in the Brahma Purana. This last argument is of weight in regard to the particular instance specified; and the designation of Sàkti may not be correctly applicable to the whole class, although it is to some of the series; for there is no incompatibility in the advocacy of Tantrika modification of the Hindu religion by any Purana; and it has unquestionably been practiced in works known as Upapuranas. The proper appropriation of the third class of the Puranas, according to the Padma Purana, appears to be the worship of Krishna, not in the character in which he is represented in the Vishnu and Bhagabata Puranas,—in which the incidents of his boyhood are only a portion of his biography, and in which the human character largely participates at least in the riper years,—but as the infant Krishna, Govinda, Bala Gopal, the sojourner in Brindavana, the companion of the cow-herd and milkmaids, the lover of Radha, or as the juvinile master of the universe, Jagannath. The term Rajasa, implying the animation of passion and enjoyment of sensual delights, is applicable not only to the character of youthful divinity, but to those with whom his adoration in the forms seems to have originated, as the Gosains of Gocul and Bengal the followers and descendants of Vallabha and Chaitanya, the priests and proprietors of Jagannath and Srinahdwar, who lead a life of affluence and indulgence, and vindicate, both by precept and practice, the reasonableness of Rajasa property, and the congruity of temporal enjoyment with the duties of religion.

THE NUMBER OF PURANAS.

Phe Puranas are uniformly stated to be eighteen in number. It is said that there are also eighteen Upapuranas or minor Puranas : but the names only of a few of those are specified in the least exception able authorities ; the greater number of the works is not procurable. With regard to the eighteen Puranas, there is a peculiarity in the specification which is proof of an interference with the integrity of the text, in some of them, at least ; for each of them specifies the names of the whole eighteen Now, the list could not have been complete whilst the work that gives was unfinished ; and in one only therefore the last of the series have we a right to look for it. As however there are more last words than one, it is evident that the names must have been inserted in all except one, after the whole were completed. Which of the eighteen is the exception, and truly the last, there is no clue to discover ; and the specification is, probably, an interpolation, in most, if not in all.

The names that are specified are commonly the same, there are as follows ; 1 Brahma, 2 Padma 3 Vaishnava, 4 Saiva, 5 Bhagabata, 6 Naradya 6 Markandeya, 8 Agneya, 9 Vavishya, 10 Brahma

Vaivarta, 11 Linga, 12 Varaha, 13 Skanda, 14 Vaman, 15 Kurma, 16 Matsya, 17 Garuda, 18 Brahmanda. This is from the twelfth book of Bhagabata, and is the same as occurs in the Vishnu In other authorities there are a few variations. The list of the Kurma Purana omits the Agni purana, and substitutes the Vayu. The Agni leaves out the Siva, and inserts the Vayu. The Baraha omits the Garuda and Brahmanda and inserts the Vayu and Narasinha; in this last it is singular. The Markandeya agrees with the Vishnu and Bhagabat in omitting the Vayu. The Matsya, like Agni leaves out the Siva.

Some of the Puranas, as the Agni, Matsya. Bhagabat, and Padma, also particularize the number of stanzas which each of the eighteen contains. In one or two instances they disagree; but, in general, they concur. The aggregate is stated at 400,000 slokas or 1,600,000 lines There are fabled to be but an abridgment, the whole amount being a krore or ten millions of stanzas or even a thousand millions. If all the fragmentary portions claiming in various parts of India, to belong to the Puranas were admitted, their extent would much exceed the lesser, though it would not reach the larger, enumeration. The former is, however, as I have elsewhere stated, a quantity that an individual European scholar could scarcely expect to persue with due care and attention, unless his whole time were devoted exculsively, for many years to the task. Yet without some such labour being achieved, it was clear, from the crudity and in exactness of all that had been hitherto published on the subject, and one exception, that sound views on the subject of Hindu mythology and tradition were not to be expected. Circumstances which I have already explained in the paper in the journal of the Royal Asiatic Society, referred to, above, enabled me to avail myself of competent assistance, by which I made a minute abstract of most of the Puranas. In course of time I hope to place tolerably copious and connected analysis of the whole eighteen before Oriental scholars, and, in the meanwhile, offer a brief notice of their several contents.

In general, the enumeration of Puranas is a simple nomenclature, with the addition in some cases, of the number of verses, but to these the Matsya Purana joins the mention of one or two circumstances, peculiar to each, which, although scanty, are of value, as offering means of identifying the copies of the Puranas now found with those to which the Matsya refers, or to discovering a difference between the present and past. I shall therefore prefix the passage destructive of each Purana, from the Matsya. It is necessary to remark however, that, in the comparison instituted between that description and the Purana as it exists, I necessarily refer the copy or copies which I employed for the purpose of examination and analysis, and which were procured, with some trouble and cost, in Benares and Calcutta. In some instances my manuscripts have been collated with others from different parts of India; and the result has shown that with regard at least to the Brahma, Vishnu, Vayu, Matsya, Padma, Bhagavat, and Kurma Puranas, the same works in all essential respects, are generally current under the same appellations. Whether this is invariably the case may be doubted; and further inquiry may possibly show that I have been obliged to content myself with mutilated or unauthentic works. It is with this reservation, therefore that I must be understood to speak of the concurrence or disagreement of any Purana with the notice of it which the Matsya Purana has preserved.

SYNOPSIS OF THE PURANAS.

1. Brahma Purana. "That the whole of which formerly repeated by Brahma to Marichi, is called

the Brahma Purana, and contains ten thousand stanzas." In all the list of the Puranas the Brahma is placed at the head of the series, and is, thence, sometimes also entitled the Adi or 'first' Purana. It is also designated as the Saura; as it is, in great part, appropriated to the worship of Saura, the sun.' There are, however, works bearing these names which belongs to the class of Upapuranas, and which are not to be confounded with the Brahma. It is usually said, as above, to contain ten thousand slokas; bnt the number actually occuring is between seven and eight thousands; there is a suplementary or concluding section, called the Brahmottara Purana, and which is different from a portion of the Skanda called the Brahmottara Khanda, which contains about three thousand stanzas more. But there is every reason to conclude that this is a distinct and unconnected work.

The immediate narrator of the Brahma Purana is Lomaharshana, who communicates it to the Rishis or revealed by Brahma, not to Marichi as the Matsya affirms, but to Daksha another of the patriarchs, Hence its denomination by the Brahma Purana.

The early chapters of the work give a description of creation, an account of the Manwantaras and the history of the solar and lunar dynasties to the time of Krishna, of a summary manner, and in words which are common to it and several other Puranas. A brief description of the universe succeeds; and then comes a number of chapters relating to the holiness of Orissa, with its temples and sacred groves dedicated to the sun, to Siva and Jagannatha, the latter specially. These chapters are characteristic of this Purana, and show its main object to be the promotion of the worship of Krishna as Jagannatha. To these particulars succeeds a life of Krishna, which is word for word the same as that of the Vishnu Purana; and the compilation terminates with a pariicular detail of the mode in which Yoga or contemplative devotion, the object of which is still Vishnu, is to be perform ed. There is a little, in this, which corresponds with the definition of a Pancha-lakshana Purana ; and the mention of the temples of Orissa, the date of the original construction of which is recorded, shows that it could not have been complied earlier than the thirteenth or fourteenth century.

The Uttara Khanda of the Brahma Purana bears still more entirely the character of a Mahatmya or local legends; being intended to celebrate the sanctity of the Balaja river, conjectured to be the same as the Banas in Marwar. There is no clue to its date but it is clearly modern; grafting personages and fictions of its own invention on a few hints from older authorities.

2. Padma Purana. That which contains an account of the period when the world was a golden lotus (Padma), and of all the occurrences of that time, is, therefore, called the Padma by the wise. It contains fifty-five thousand stanzas. The second Purana, in the usual list, is always the Padma, a very voluminous work, containing, according to its own statement, as well as that of other authorities, fifty-five thousand slokas: an amount not far from the truth. These are divided amongst five books or Khandas: 1. The Srishti Khanda or section of creation; 2. The Bhumi Khanda, description of the earth; 3. The Swarga Khanda, chapter on heaven; 4. Patal Khanda chapter on the reign below the earth; and 5. The Uttara Khanda, last or supplementary chapter. There is also current a sixth division, the Kriya Yoga Sara, a treatise on the practice of devotion. The denominations of the divisions of the Padma Purana convey but an imperfect and impartial notion of their contents. In the first section which treats of creation, the natrator is Ugrasravas, the suta, the son of Lomharshana, who is sent, by his father to the Rishis at Naimisharanaya, to com-

municate to them Purana, which, from its containing an account of the lotus (padma) in which Brahma appeared at creation, is termed the Padma, or Padma Purana. The suta repeats what was originally communicated by Brahma to Pulastya, and by him to Bhishma. The early chapters narrate the cosmogony, and the genealogy of the patriarchal families, much in the same style, and often in the same words, as the Vishnu; and short accounts of Manwantaras and legal dynasties but these, which are legitimate Pauranic matters, soon make way for new and unauthentic inventions, illustrative of the virtue of the lake of Puskara or Pokher in Ajmir, as a place of pilgrimage.

The Bhumi Khanda, or section of the earth, defers any description of the earth until near its close; filling up one hundred and twenty-seven chapters with legends of a very mixed description, some ancient, and common with other Puranas, but the greater part peculiar to itself, illustrated by Tirthas, either figuratively so termed,—as a wife, a parent, or a Guru, considered as a sacred object,—or places to which actual pilgrimage should be performed.

The Swarga Khanda describes in the first chapters, the relative positions of the Lokas or spheres above the earth; placing above all,

Vaikuntha, the sphere of Vishnu, an addition which is not warranted by what appears to be the oldest cosmogony. Miscellaneous notices of some of the most celebrated princes then succeed, conformably to the usual narratives; and they are followed by rules of conduct for the several castes, and at different stages of life. The rest of the book is occupied by legends of diversified description, introduced with much method or contrivance; a few of which, as Daksha's sacrifice, are of ancient date, but of which the most are original and modern.

The Patal Khanda devotes a brief introduction to the description of Patal, the regions of the snake gods. But the name of Rama having been mentioned, Sesha, who has succeeded Pulastya as spokesman, proceeds to narrate the history of Rama, his descendants, and his posterity; in which the compiler seems to have taken the poem of Kalidasa, the Raghu Vamsa, for his chief authority. An originality of addition may be suspected, however in the adventures of the horse destined by Rama for an Aswamedha, which forms the subject of a great many chapters. When about to be sacrificed, the horse turns out to be a Brahman, condemned by an imprecation of Durvasa, a sage, to assume the equine nature, and who by having been sanctified by coneection with Rama, is released from his metamorphosis, and despatched as a spirit of light, to heaven. This piece of Vaishnava fiction is followed by praises of Sri Bhagavata, an account of Krishna's juvenilities, and the merits of worshipping Vishnu. These accounts are communicated through a machinery borrowed from the Tantras: they are told by Sadasiva to Parvati, the ordinary interlocutors of Tantrika compositions.

The Uttara Khanda is a most voluminous aggregation of very heterogenous matters, but it is consistent in adopting a decidedly Vaishnava tone, and admitting no compromise with any other form of faith. The chief subjects are first discussed in a dialogue between king Dilip and the Muni Vasistha, such as the merits of bathing in the month of Magha, and the potency of the Mantra or prayer addressed to Laksmi Narayana. But the nature of Bhakti, faith in Vishnu—the use of Vaishnava marks on the body—the legends of Vishnu's Avataras, and especially of Rama—and the construction of images of Vishnu—are too important to be left to mortal discretion. They are explained by Siva to Parvati, and wound up by the adoration of Vishnu by those divinities. The dialogue then reverts to the king and the sage and the latter states why Vishnu is the only one of the triad entitled to respect, Siva being licentious, Brahma arrogant, and Vishnu alone pure. Vasistha then repeats, after Siva, the Mahatmya of the Bhagavata Gita; the merit of each book of which is illustrated by legends of the good consequences, to individuals, from persuing or hearing it. Other Vaishnava Mahatmyas occupy considerable portions of this Khanda, especially the Karttika Mahatmya, or holiness of the month of Karttika, illustrated, as usual by stories, a few of which are of an earlier origin, but the greater part of modern, and peculiar to this Purana.

The Kriya Yoga Sara is repeated by Suta, to the Rishis, after Vyasa's communication of it to Jaimini, in an answer to an inquiry how religious merit might be secured in the Kali age, in which men have become incapable of the penances and abstraction by which final liberation was formerly to be attained. The answer is, of course, that which is intimated in the last book of the Vishnu Purana—personal devotion to Vishnu. Thinking of him, repeating his names, wearing his marks, worshipping in his temples, are a full substitute for all other acts of moral, or devotional, and contemplative, merit.

The different portions of Padma Purana are

in all probablity, as many different works, neither of which approaches to the original definition of a Purana. There may be some connexion between the three first portions, at least as to time: but there is no reason to consider them as of high antiquity. They specify the Jainas, both by name and practices; they talk of Mlechchas, "barbarians," flourishing in India; they command the use of the frontal and other Vaishnava marks; and they notice other subjects which, like these, are of no romote origin. The Patal Khanda dwells copiously upon the Bhagabat, and is consequently posterior to it. The Uattra Khanda is intolerably Vaishnava, and is therefore unquestionably modern. It enjoins the veneration of the Salagrama stone and Tulsi plant, the use of the Tapta-mudra, or stamping with a hot iron the name of Vishnu on the skin, and a variety of practices and observances undoubtedly no part of the original system. It speaks of the shrines of Sriranga and Venkadatri in the Dekkan, temples that have no pretension to remote antiquity; and it names Haripura on the Tungabhadra, which is in likelihood, the city of Vijayanagara, founded in the middle of the fourteenth century. The Kriya Yoga Sara is equally a modern, and apparently, a Bengali composition. No portion of the

Padma Purana is, probably, older than the twelfth century; and the last parts may be as recent as the fifteenth or sixteenth.

3. Vishnu Purana. "That in which Parasara, beginning with the events of the Varaha Kalpa, expounds all duties, is called the Vaishnava: and the learned know its extent to be twenty-three thousand stanzas. It may be here observed, however, that the actual member of verses contained in it falls far short of the enumeration of the Matsya, with which the Bhagabata concurs. Its actual contents are not seven thousand stanzas. All the copies and, in this instance, they are not fewer than seven in number,—procured both in the east and in the west of India, agree; and there is no appearance of any part being wanting. There is a beginning, a middle, and an end, in both text and comment; and the work, as it stands, is, incontestably, entire. How is the discrepancy to be explained?,

4. Vayu Purana. The Purana in which Vayu has declared the laws of duty, in connection with the Sweta Kalpa, and which comprises the Mahatmya of Rudra, is the Vayaviya Purana: it contains twenty-four thousand verses. The Siva or Siva Purana is, as above remarked, omitted in some of the lists; and, in general, when that is the case, it is replaced by the Vayu or Vayaviya.

When the Siva is specified, as in the Bhagabata, then the Vayu is omitted; intimating the possible identity of these two works. This, indeed, is confirmed by the Matsya, which describes the Vayaviya Purana as characterised by its account of the greatness of the Rudra or Siva: and Balam Bhatta mentions that the Vayaviya is also called the Siva, though, according to some, the latter is the name of the Upapurana. Colonel Vans Kennedy observes, that, in the west of India, the Siva is considered to be an Upapurana or minor Purana.

Another proof that the same work is intended by the authorities here followed, the Bhagabata and Matsya, under different appellations, is their concurrence in the extent of the work; each specifying its verses to be twenty-four thousand. A copy of the Siva Purana, of which an index and analysis have been prepared, does not contain more than about seven shousand. It cannot therefore, be the Siva Purana of the Bhagabata: and we may safely consider that to be the same as the Vayaviya of the Matsya.

The Vayu Purana is narrated, by Suta, to the Rishis at Naimisharanya, as it was formerly told, at the same place, to similar persons, by Vayu; a repetition of circumstances not uncharacteristic of the inartificiai style of this Purana. It is divided into four Padas, termed, severally, Prakriya, Upadghata, Anushanga, and Upasambara; a classification peculiar to this work. These are preceded by an index, or heads of chapters, in the manner of the Mahabharata and Ramayana—another peculiarity.

The Prakriya portion contains but a few chapters and treats, chiefly, of elemental creation and the first evolutions of beings to the same purport as the Vishnu, but in a more obscure and unmethodical style. The Upodghata then continues the subject of creation and describes the various Kalpas or periods during which the world has existed; a greater number of which is specified by the Siva, than by the Vaishnava Puranas. Thirty-three are here described, the last of which is the Sweta or white 'Kalpa,' from Siva's being born in it, of a white complexion. Then geneologies of the patriarchs, the description of the universe, and the incidents of the first six Manwantaras are all treated of in this part of the work: but they are intermixed with legends and praises of Siva as the sacrifice of Daskha, the Maheswara Mahatmya, the Nilakanta stotra, and others. The geneologies, although, in the main, the same as those in the Vaishnava Puranas, present some variations. A long account of the Pitris or progenitors is also peculiar to the Purana; as are stories of some of the most celebrated Rishis who are engaged in the distribution of the Vedas.

The third division commences with an account of the seven Rishis and their descendants, and describes the origin of the different classes of creatures from the daughter of Daksha, with a profuse copiousness of nomenclature, not found in any other Purana. With the exception of the greater minuteness of detail, the particulars agree with those of the Vishnu Purana. A chapter then occurs on the worship of Pitris; another on Tirthas or places sacred to them; and several on the performance of Sraddhas, constituting the Sraddha Kalpa. After this comes a full account of the solar and lunar dynasties, forming a parallel to that in the following pages, with this difference, that it is throughout, in verses, whilst that of our text, as noticed in its place, is, chiefly in prose. It is extended, also, by the insertion of detailed accounts of virtuous incidents, briefly noticed in Vishnu, though derived, apparently, from a common original. The section terminates with similar accounts of future kings, and the same chronological calculations, that are found in the Vishnu.

The last portion, the Upasamhara describes briefly the future Manwantaras, the measures of space and time, the end of the world, the efficacy of Yoga, and the glories of Sivapura, or the dwelling of the Siva, with whom the Yogin is to be united. The manuscript concludes with a different history of the successive teachers of the Vayu, Purana, tracing them from Brahma to Vayu, from Vayu to Brihaspati, and from him, through various deities and sages, to Dwaipayana and Sutta.

The account given of this Purana in the journal of the Asiatic Society of Bengal was limited to something less than half the work; as I had not then been able to procure a large portion I have now a more complete one of my own; and there are several copies in the East India Company's library, of the like extent. One presented by His Highness the Gaikwar, is dated Samvat 1540 or A.D., 1482, and is evidently, as old as it professed to be. The examination I have made of the work confirms the view I formerly took of it; and, from the internal evidence it affords, it may perheps, be regarded as one of the oldest and most authentic specimens, extant, of a primitive Purana.

It appears, however, that we have not yet a copy of the entire Vayu Purana. The extent of it as mentioned above, should be twenty four thousand verses. The Gaikwar's Ms. has but twelve thousand, and is denominated the Purvardha or first portion. My copy is of the like extent. The index also shows, that several subjects remain untold; as, subsequently to the description of the sphere of Siva, and the periodical dissolution of the world, the work is said to contain an account of a succeeding creation, and of various events that occured in it, as the birth of several celebrated Rishis including that of Vyasa, and a description of his distribution of the Vedas; an account of the enmity between Vasistha and Vishwamitra; and a Naimisharanaya Mahatmya. These tropics are, however, of minor importance, and can scarcely carry the Purana to the whole extent of the verses which it is said to contain. In the number is accurate, the index must still omit a considerable portion of the subsequent contents.

5. Sri Bhagavata Purana. "That in which ample details of duty are described, and which opens with (an extract from) the Gayatri; that in which the death of the Asura Vritra' is told, and in which the mortals and immortals of the Saraswati Kalpa, with the events that happened to them in the world, are related: that is celebrated as the Bhagavata, and consists of eighteen thousand verses." Bhagavata is a work of great celebrity in India, and exercises a more direct and powerful influence upon the opinions and

feelings of the people than, perhaps, any other of the Puranas. It is placed the fifth in all the lists; but the Padma Purana ranks it as the eighteenth, as the extracted substance of all the rest. According to the usual specification it consists of eighteen thousand Slokas, distributed amongst three hundred and thirty-two chapters divided into twelve Skandas or books. It is named Bhagavata from its being dedicated to the glorification of Bhagavata or Vishnu.

The Bhagagata is communicated to the Rishis at Naimisharanya by Suta, as usual: but he only repeats what was narrated by Suka, the son of Vyasa, to Parikshit the king of Hastinapur, the grandson of Arjuna. Having incurred the imprecation of a hermit, by which he sentenced to die of the bite of a venomous snake at the expiration of seven days, the king, in preparation for this event, repairs to the banks of the Ganges, whither also come the gods, sages to witness his death. Amongst the latter is Suka: and it is in reply to Parikshit's question; what a man should do who is about to die, that he narrates the Bhagavata. as he had heard it from Vyasa: for nothing secures final happiness so certainly, as to die whilst the thoughts are wholly engrossed by Vishnu.

The course of the narration opens with a cosmogony, which although, in most respects similar to that of other Puranas, is more largely intermixed with allegory and mysticism, and drives its tone more from the Vedanta than the Sankhya philosophy. The doctrine of active creation by the supreme, as one with Vasudeva, is more distinctly asserted, with a decided enunciation of the effects being resolvable into Maya or illusion. There are also, doctrinal peculiaries highly characteristic of this Purana, amongst which he assertion, that it was originally communicated by Brahma to Narada, that all men whatsoever, Hindus of every caste, and even Mlechchas, out-castes or barbarians, might learn to have faith in Vasudeva.

In the third book, the interlocutors are changed to Maitreya or Vidur, the former of whom is the disciple in the Vishnu Purana; the latter was the half-brother of the Kuru princes. Maitreya again gives an account of the Shristi-lilâ, or sport of creation, in a strain partly common to the Puranas partly peculiar; although he declares he learned it from his teacher Parasara, at the desire of Pulastya referring, thus, to the fabulous origin of the Vishnu Purana and furnishing evidence of its priority. Again however, the authority is changed; and the narrative is said to have been that which was communicated by Sesha to the Nagas The creation of Brahma is then described, and the divistons of time are explained. A very long and peculiar account is given of the Varaha incarnation of Vishnu, which is followed by the creation of the Prajapati and Swayambhuva whose daughter Devahuti is married to Kardama Rishi, an incident peculiar to this work, as that follows, the Avatara of Vishnu, as Kalpa the son of Kardama and Devahuti the author of the Sankhya philosophy, which he expounded after a Vaishnava fashion, to his mother in the last nine chapters of this section.

The Manwantaras of Swayambhuva, and the multiplication of the patriarchal families, are next described with some peculiarities of nomenclature. The traditions of Dhruba, Venn, Prithu, and other princes in ihe period, are the other subjects of the fourth Skandha, and are continued in the fifth, to that of the Varata who obtained emancipation. The details generally conform to those of the Vishnu Purana; and the same words are often employed; so that it would be difficult to determine which work had the best right to them, had not the Bhagavata itself indicated its obligation to the Vishnu. The remainder of the fifth book is occupied with the description of the universe; and the same conformity which the Vishnu continues.

This is only partially the cause with the sixth book, which contains a variety of legends of a miscellaneous description, intended to illustrate the merit of worshiphing Viahnu. Some of them belong to the early stock; but some apparently novel. The seventh book is, mostly occupied with the legends of Prahlada. In the eighth, we have an account of the remaining Manwantaras; in which, as happening in the course of them, a variety of ancient legends are repeated, as the battle between the king of the elephants and an alligator, the churning of the ocean, and the dwarf and fish Avataras. heT ninth book narrates the dynasties of the Vaivaswata Manwantara,tor the prince of the solar and lunar races to the time of Krishna. The particulars conform, generally, with those recorded in the Vishnu.

The tenth book is the characteristic part of this Purana, and the portion upon which its popularity is founded. It is appropriated entirely to the history of Krishna, which it narrates much in the same manner as the Vishnu, but in more detail; holding a middle place, however, between it and the extravagant prolixity with which the Harivamsa repeats the story. It is not necessary to particularize it further. It has been translated into, perhaps, all the languages in India, and it a favourite work with all descriptions of people.

The eleventh book describes the destruction of the Yadavas and the death of Krishna. Previous to the latter event, Krishna instructs Uddhava in the performance of Yoga; a snbject consigned by the Vishnu, to the concluding passages. The narrative is much the same, but something more summary than that of the Vishnu. The twelfth book continues the lines of the kings of the Kali age prophetically, to a similar period as Vishnu, and gives a like account of the deterioration of all things and their final dissolution.

Consistently with the subject of the Purana, the serpent Takshaka bites Parikshit, and he expires and the work should terminate; or the close might be extended to the subsequent sacrtfice of Janamejaya, for the destruction of the whole serpent race. There is a rather awkwardly introduced description however of the arrangement of the Vedas and Puranas by Vyasa, and the legend of Markandeya's interview with the infant Krishna, during a period of worldly dissolution. We then come to the end of the Bhagavata in a series of encomiastic commendations of its own sanctity and efficacy to salvation.

Mr. Colebrooke observes of the Bhagavata Purana, "I am, myself, inclined to adopt an opinion supported by many learned Hindus, who consider the celebratəd Sri Bhagavata as the work of a grammarian [Bopedeva] supposed to have lived about six hundred years ago." Colonel Vans Kennedy considers this an incautions admission, because "it is unquestionable that the number of the Puranas has been always held to the eighteen; but in most of the Puranas the names of the eighteen are enumerated, amongst which the Bhagavata is invariably included; and consequently, if it were composed only six hundred years ago, the others must be of an equally modern date." Some of them are no doubt more recent; but as already remarked no weight can be attached to the specification of eighteen names; for they are always complete; each Purana enumerates all. Which is the last? which had the opportunity of naming its seventeen predecessors, and adding itself? The argument proves too much. There can be little doubt that the list has been inserted, upon the authority of tradition either by some improving transcriber, or by the complier of a work more recent than the eighteen genuine Puranas. The object is also reputed by the assertion, that there was another Purana to which the name applies, and which is still to be met with the Devi Bhagavata.

For the authenticity of the Bhngavata is one of the few questions, affecting their sacred literature, which Hindu writers have ventured to discuss. The occasion is furnished by the text itself. In the fourth chapter of the first book, it is said that Vyasa arranged the Vedas, and divided them into four, and that he then complied the Itihasa and Puranas, as a fifth Veda. The Vedas he gave to Paila and the rest; the Itihasa and Puranas, to Lomarshana, the father of Suta. Then, reflecting that these works may not be accessible to women, Sudras,and mixed castes, he composed the Bharata for the purpose of placing religious knowledge within their reach. Still, he felt dissatisfied, and wandered, in much perplexity, along the banks of the Saraswati, where his hermitage was situated while Narada paid him a visit. Having confided to him his secret and seemingly causeless dissatisfaction, Narada suggested that it arose from his not having sufficiently dwelt, in the works he had finished, upon the merit of worshipping Vasudeva. Vyasa at once admitted its truth, and found a remidy for his uneasiness in the composition of Bhagavata, which he taught to Suka. his son. There, therefore, is the most positive assertion that the Bhagavata was composed subsequently to the Puranas and given to a different pupil, and was not, therefore, one of the eighteen of which Romaharshana the Suta, was, according to all concurrent testimonies, the depositary. Still the Bhagavat is named amongst, the eighteen Puranas, by the inspired authorities: and how can these incongruities be reconciled.

The principal point of dispute seems to have been started by an expression of Shridhara Swamin a commantator on the Bhagavata, who somewhat incautiously made the remark, that there was no reason to suspect that by the term Bhagavata, any other work than the subject of his labours was meant. This was therefore, an admission that some suspicious had been entertained of the correctness of the nomenclature, and that an opinion had been expressed, that the term belonged, not to the Sri Bhagavata, but to the Devi Bhagavata; to a Saiva, not a Vaishnava composition. With whom doubts prevailed prior to Sridharr Swamin, or by whom they were urged, does not appear; for as far as we are aware, no works anterior to his date in which they are advanced, having been written on the subject. There are three in the library of the East India Company, the Durjana Mukha Chapetika. 'A slap of the face for the vile,' by Romasrama; the Durjana Mukha Maha Chapetika.' A great slap of the face for the wicked,' by Kasinath Bhatta; and the Durjana Mukha Padma Paduka. 'A slipper for the same part of the same persons, by a nameless disputant. The first maintains the authenticity of the Bhagavata; second asserts, that Devi Bhagavata is the genuine Purana; and the third replied to the arguments of the first. There is, also, a work by Purushathama, entitled. 'Thirteen arguments for dispelling all doubts of the character of the Bhagavata' (Bhagavata Swarupa Vishya Sanka Nirasa Trayadasa); whilst Balam Bhatta, a commentator on the Mitakshara, indulging in a dissertation on the meaning of the word Purana, adduces reason for questioning the inspired origin of this Purana.

The insertion of a Bhagavata amongst the eighteen Puranas is acknowledged; but this, it is said, can be the Devi Bhagavata alone: for the circumstances apply more correctly to it than to Vaishnava Bhagavata. Thus, a text is quoted, by Kasinatha, from a Purana—he does not state which that says, of the Bhagavata, that it contains eighteen thousand verses, twelve books, and three hundred and thirty-two chapters. Kasinatha asserts that the chapters of the Sri Bhagavata are three hundred and thirty-five, and that the numbers apply, throughout, only to the Devi Bhagavata. It is also said that the Bhagavata contains an account of the acquirement of holy knowledge by Hayagriva, the particulars of the Saraswata Kalpa; a dialogue between

Ambarisha and Suka; and that it commences with the Gayatri, or, at least, a citation of it. These all apply to the Devi Bhagavata alone, except the last; but it also is more true of the Saiva than of the Vaishnava work; for the latter has only one word of the Gayatri, dhimahi, 'we meditate,' whilst the former to dhimahi adds, yo nah' prachodayat 'who may enlighten us.' To the third argument it is, in the first place, objected, that the citation of the Bhagavata by modern writers is no test of its authenticity; and, with regard to the more ancient commentary of Sankara Acharya, it is said, "Where is it?" Those who advocate the sanctity of the Bhagavata reply: "It was written in difficult style, and became obsolete, and is last." A very unsatisfactory plea, retort their opponents; "for we still have the works of Sankara, several of which are quite as difficult as any in the Sanskrit language." The existence, of this comment, too rests upon the authority of Madhwa, or Madhava, who, in a commentary of his own, asserts that he has consulted eight others. Now, amonst these is one by the monkey Hanumat; and, although a Hindu disputant may believe in the reality of such a composition, yet we may receive its citation as a proof that Madhwa was not very scrupulous in the verification of authorities.

There are other topics urged, in this controversy on both sides, some of which are simple enough, some are ingenious: but the statement of the next is, of itself, sufficient to show, that, according to the received opinion, of all the authorities, of the priority of the eighteen Puranas, to the Bharata, it is possible that the Sri Bhagavata, which is subsequent to the Bharata, should be of the number; and the evidence of style, the superiority of which to that of the Puranas in general is admitted by the disputants, is also a proof that it is the work of a different hand. Whether the Devi Bhagavata has a better title to be considered as an original composition of Vyasa, is equally question; but it can not be doubted that the Sri Bhagavata is the product of uninspired erudition. There does not seem to be any other ground than tradition for ascribing it to Bopadeva the grammarian: but there is no reason to call the tradition in question. Bopadeva flourished at the court of Hemadri, Raja of Devagiri, Deogur or Dowlatabad, and must, consequently, have lived prior to the conquest of that principality by the Mahomadans in the fourteenth century. The death of twelth century, commonly assigned to him, is, probably, correct, and is that of the Bhagavat Purana.

6. Narada or Naradiya Purana. Where Narada

has described the duties which were observed in the Brihat Kalpa, that is called the Naradiya, having twenty-five thousand stanzas. If the number of verses be here correctly stated, the Purana has not fallen into my hands. The copy I have analysed contains, not many more than three thousand slokas. There is another work which might be expected to be of greater extent, the Brihan Naradiya or great Narada Purana; but this, according to the concurrence of three copies in my possession, and of five others in the Company's library, contains but about three thousand five hundred verses. It may be doubted, therefore, if the Narada Purana of the Matsya exists.

According to the Matsya, the Narada Purana is related by Narada, and gives an account of the Brihat Kalpa. The Naradiya Purana is communicated, by Narada, to the Rishis at Naimisharanya on the Gomati river. The Brihan Naradiya is related to the same persons, at the same place, by Suta, as it was told by Narada to Sanatkumar. Possibly, the term 'Brihat' may have been suggested by the specification which is given in the Matsya: but there is no description, in it, of any particular Kalpa or day of Brahma.

From a cursory examination of the Puranas it is very evident that they have no conformity to the defination of a Purana, and that both are sectarial and modern compilations, intended to support the doctrine of Vakti or faith in Vishnu. With this view, they have collected a variety of prayers addressed to one or other form of that divinity; a number of observances and holidays connected with his adoration; different legends some, perhaps, of an early, others of a more recent date, illustrative of efficacy of devotion to Hari. Thus, in the Narada, we have the stories of Dhruva and Prahlada; the latter told in the words of Vishnu: whilst the second portion of it is occupied with a legend of Mohini, the well-born daughter of a king called Rukmangala; beguiled by whom, the king offers to perporm for her whatever she may desire. She calls upon him either to violate the rule of fasting on the eleventh day of the fort-night, a day sacred to Vishnu, or put his son to death; and he kills his son, as the lesser sin of the two. This shows the spirit of the work. Its date may also be inferred from its tenor; as such mons-trous extravagances in a praise of Bhakti are, cer-tainly, of modern origin. One limit it furnishes, itself; for it refers to Suka and Parikshit, the inter-locutors of the Bhagavata; and it is consequently, subsequent to the date of the Purana. It is pro-bably, considerably later; for it affords evidence that it was written after India was in the hands of the Mahomedans. In the concluding passage it is said: "Let not this Purana be repeated in the presence of the 'killers of cows' and contemners of the gods." It is, possibly, a compilation of the sixteenth or seventeenth century.

The Brihan Naradiya is a work of the same tenor and time. It contains little else than penegyrical prayers addressed to Vishnu, and injunctions to observe various rites, and keep holy certain seasons, in honour of him. The earlier legends introduced are the birth of Markandeya, the destruction of Sagara's sons, and the dwarf Avatara, but they are subservient to the design of the whole, and are rendered occasions for praising Narayana. Others, illustrating the efficacy of certain Vaishnava observances, are purile inventions, wholly foreign to the more ancient system of Pauranik fiction. There is no attempt at cosmogony, or patriarchal or regal geneology. It is possible that those topics may be treated of in the missing stanzas: but it seems more l kely that the Narada Purana of the lists has little in common with the words to which its name is applied in Bengal and Hindusthan.

7. Markanda or Markandeya Purana. "That Purana in which, commencing with the story of the birds that were acquainted with right and wrong

every thing is narrated fully by Markandeya, as it was explained by holy sages, in reply to the question of the Muni, is called the Markandeya, containing nine thousand verses." This is so called from its being, in the first instance, narrated by Markandeya Muni, and, in the second place, by certain fabulous birds; thus far agreeing with the account given of it in the Matsya. Thus as well as other authorities, specify its containing nine thousand stanzas; but my copy closes with a verse affirming that the number of verses recited by the Muni was six thousand nine hundred; and a copy in the East India Company's library has a similar specification. The termination, is, however, somewhat abrupt; and there is no reason why the subject with which it ends should not have been carried on further. One copy in the Company's library, indeed belonging to the Guiekwar's collection, states, at the close, that it is the end of the first Kanda or section. If the Purana was ever completed, the remaining portion of it appears to be lost.

Jaimini, the pupil of Vyasa, applies to Markandeya to be made acquainted with the nature of Vasudeva, and for an explanation of some of the incidents described in the Mahabharata; with the ambrosia of which divine poem, Vyasa, he declares has westered the whole world: a reference which establishes the priority of the Bharata to the Markandeya Purana, however incompatible this may be with the tradition, that, having finished the Puranas Vyasa wrote the poem.

Markandeya excuses himself saying he has a religious rite to perform; and he refers Jaimini to some very sapient birds who resides in the Vindhya mountains; birds of celestials origin, found, when just born by the Muni Samika, on the field of Kuru kshetra, and brought up by him, along with his scholars; in consequence of which, and by virtue of their heavenly descent, they be came profoundly versed in the Vedas and a knowledge of sairitual truth. This machinery is borrowed from the Mahabharat, with some embellishment. Jaimini, accordlingly, has recourse to the birds, Pingaksha and his brethern, and puts to them the questions he had asked of the Muni: "Why was Vasudeva born as a mortal? How was it that Draupadi was the wife of the five Pandavas? Why did Baladeva do penance for Brahmanicida? And why were the children of Draupadi destroyed, when they had Krishna and Arjuna to defend them?" The answers to these inquiries occupy a number of chapters, and form a sort of supplement to the Mahabharata; supplying, partly by invention, perhaps and partly by reference to equally ancient authorities, the blanks left in some of its narrations.

Legends of Britrasura's death, Baladeva's penance, Harish Chandra's elevation to heaven, and the quarrel between Vasistha and Vishwakarma,are followed by a discussion respecting birth, death and sin; which leads to a more extended description of the different hells than is found in other Puranas. The account of creation which is contained in the work is repeated by the birds, after Markandeya's account of it to Kraushtuki, and confined to the origin of the Vedas and patriarchal families, amongst whom are new characters, as Daksha and his wife Marshiti, and their descendants; allegorical personages, representing intolerable iniquity and its consequence. There is then a description of the world, with, as usual to this Purana, several singularities, some of which are noticed in the following pages. This being the state of the world in the Swayambhu Manwantara an account of the other Manwantaras succeeds, in which the birth of the Manus, and a number of other particulars are peculiar to this work. The present or Vaivaswata Manwantara is very briefly passed over; but the next, the first of the future Manwantaras contains the long episodical narrative of the actions of the goddess Durga, which is the special boast of this Purana, and is the text book of the worshippers of Kali, Chandi, or Durga, in Bengal. It is the Chandi Patha, or Durga Mahatmya in which the victories of the goddess over different evil beings or Asuras are detailed with considerable power and spirit. It is read daily in the temples of Durga, and furnishes the pomp and circumstances of the great festival ot Bengal, the Doorga Pooja, public worship of that Goddess.

After the account of the Manwantaras is completed, there follows a series of legends, some new, some old relating to the sun and his posterity; contaiued to Vaivaswata Manu and his sons, and their immediate descendants; terminating with Dama, the son of Narishyanta. Of most of the persons noticed the work narrates particulars not found elsewhere.

This Purana has a character different from that of all the others. It has nothing of a sectarial spirit, little of a religious tone; rarely inserting prayers and invocations to any deity; and such as are inserted are brief and moderate. It deals little in precepts, ceremonial or moral. Its leading feature is narative; and it presents an uninterrupted succession of legends, most of which, when ancient, are embellished with new circumstances, and when new, partake so far of the spirit of the old, that they are disinterested creations of the imagination, having no particular motive being designed to recommend no special doctrine or observance. Whether they are derived from any other source, or whether they are original inventions, it is not possible to ássertain. They are, most probably, for the greater part, at least original; and the whole has been narrated in the compiler's own manner, a manner superior to that of the Puranas in general. with exception of the Bhagavata.

It is not easy to conjecture a date for this Purana. That it is subsequent, is doubtful. It is, unquestionably, more ancient than such works as the Brahma Purana, and, Naradiya Purana; and its freedom from sectarial bias is a reason for supposing it anterior to the Bhagavata. At the same time its partial conformity to the definition of a Purana, and the tenor of the additions which it has made to received legends and traditions, indicate a not very remote age; and, in the absence of any guide to a more positive conclusion, it may, conjecturally, be placed in the ninth or tenth century.

8. Agni Purana. "The Purana which describes the occurances of the Isana Kalpa, and was related by Agni to Vasistha, is called Agneya. It consists of sixteen thousand stanzas. The Agni or Agneya Purana derives its name from its having

been communicated, originally, by Agni, the deity of fire, to the Muni Vasistha, for the purpose of instructing him in the two-fold knowledge of Brahma. By him it was taught to Vyasa, who imparted it to Suta; and the latter is represented as repeating it to the Rishis at Naimisharanya. Its contents are variously specified as sixteen thousand, fifteen thousand, or fourteen thousand stanzas. The two copies of which were employed by me contain about fifteen thousand slokas. There are two, in the company's library, which do not extend to twelve thousand verses; but they are, in many other respects different from mine. One of them was written at Agra, in the reign of Akbar, in A. D. 1859.

The Agni Purana, in the form in which it has been obtained in Bengal and Benares, presents a striking contrast to the Markandeya. It may be doubted if a single line of it is original. A very great proportion of it may be traced to other sources; and a more careful collation—if the task was worth the time it would require—would probably discover the remainder.

The early chapters of this Purana describe the Avataras, and in those of Rama and Krishna, avowedly follow the Ramayana and Mahabharata. A considerable portion is appropriated to instructions for the performance of religious ceremonies; many of which belong to the Tantrika rituals and are apparently transcribed from the principal authorities of that system. Some belong to mystical forms of Saiva worship, little known in Hindusthan, though perhaps, still practised in the south. One of these is the Diksha or initiation of a novice; by which with numerous ceremonies and invocation, in which the mysterious monosyllables of Tantras are constantly repeated, the disciple is transformed into a living personation of Siva, and receives, in that capacity, the homage of his Guru, Interspersed with these are chapters descriptive of the earth and of the universe, which are same as those of the Vishnu Purana; and Mahatmyas or legends of the holy places, particularly of Gaya. Chapters on the duties of kings and on the art of war then occur, which have the appearance of being extracted from some older work, as is, undoubtedly, the chapter on judicature, which follows them, and which is the same as the text of the Mitakshara. Subsequent to these we have an account of the distribution and arrangement of the Vedas and Puranas and, in a chapter on gifts, we have a description of the Puranas, which is precisely the same and in the same situation, as the similar subject in the Matsya Purana. The geneological chapters are meagre lists, differing, in a few respects, from those commonly received, as hereafter noticed, but unaccompanied by any particulars such as those recorded or invented in the Merkandeya. The next snbject is medicine, compiled, avowedly, but injudiciously, from the Susruta. A series of chapters on the mystic worship of Siva and Devi follows; and the work winds up with a treatise on rhetoric, prosody, and grammar, according to the Sutras, of Pingala and Panini.

The cyclopadical character of the Agni Puranas, as it ts now described, excludes it from any legitimate claims to be regarded as a Purana, and proves that its origin cannot be very remote. It is subsequent to the Itihasas, to the chief work on grammar, rhetoric, and medicine, and to the introduction of the Tantrika worship of Devi. When this latter took place, is yet far from determined; but there is very probability that it dates long after the beginning of our era.

The materials of the Agni Purana are, however, no doubt, of some antiquity. The medicine of Susruta is considerably older than the ninth century; and the grammar of Panini probably precedes Christianity. The chapters on archery and arms, and on regal administration, are also distinguished by an entirely Hindu character, and must have been written long anterior to the Mahomedan invasion. So far the Agni Purana is valuable, as embodying and, preserving relics of antiquity, although compiled at a more recent date.

Colonel Wilford has made great use of a list of kings derived from an appendix to the Agni Purana, which professes to be the sixty-third or last section. As he observes, it is seldom found annexed to the Purana. I have never met with it, and doubt its ever having formed any part of the original compilation. It would appear, from Colonel Wilford's remarks that this list notices Mahammed as the institutor of an era but his account of this is not very distinct. It mentions, explicitly, however, that the list speaks of Salivahan and Vikramaditya and this is quite sufficient to establish its character. The compilers of the Puranas were not such bunglers as to bring within their chronology as well known a personage as Vikramaditya. There are, in all, parts of India, various compilations ascribed to the Puranas, which never formed any portion of their contents, and which although offering sometimes, usefull local information, and valuable as preserving popular traditions, are not, in justice, to be confounded with the Puranas, so as to cause to them to be charged with even more serious errors and anachronisms than those of which they are guilty.

The two copies of this work in the library of the East India Company appropriate the first half to a description of the ordinary and occasional observances of the Hindus, interspersed with a few legends. The latter half treats exclusively of the history of Rama.

9. Bhavishya Purana. "The Purana in which Brahma, having described the greatness of the sun, explained to Manu the existence of the world, and the characters of all created things, in the course of the Aghore Kalpa, that is called the Bhavishya; the stories being for the most part, the events of a future period. It contains fourteen thousand five hundred stanzas." This Purana, as the name implies, should be a book of prophecies, foretelling what will be (Bhavishyati), as the Matsya Purana intimates. Whether such a work exists, is doubtful. The copies, which appear to be entire, and of which there are three in the library of the East India Company, agreeing in their contents, with two in my possession, contain about seven thousand stanzas. There is another work, entitled the Bhavishyattara, as if it was a continuation or supplement of the former, containing, also, about seven thousand verses, but the subjects of both

these works are but a very imperfect degree analogus to these to which the Matsya alludes.

The Bhavishya Purana, as I have it, is a work in a hundred and twenty-six short chapters, repeated by Sumantu to Santanika, as king of the Pandu family. He notices, however its having originated with Swayambhu or Brahma, and describes it as consisting of five parts; four dedicated, it should seem, to as many deities, as they are termed. Brahma, Vaishnava, Saiva, and Twashtra; whilst the fifth is the Partisharga or repeated creation. Possibly, the first part only may have come into my hands; although it does not so appear by the manuscript.

Whatever it may be, the work in question is not a Purana. The first portion, indeed, treats of creation; but it is little else than a transcript of the words of the first chapter of Manu. The rest is entirely a manual religious rites and ceremonies. It explains the ten Samskaras or initiatary rites; the performance of the Sandhya; the reverence to be shown to a Guru; the duties of the diffierent Asramas and castes; and enjoins a number of Vratas or observances of fasting and the like, appropriate to diflerent lunar days. A few legends enliven the series of precepts. That of the sage Chyavana is told at considerable length, taken, chiefly, from the Mahabharata. The Naga Panchami, or fifth lunation sacred to the serpent Gods, gives rise to a description of differents sorts of snakes. After which occupy about one third of the chapters, the remainder of them conform, in subject, to one of the topics referred to by the Matsya. They chiefly represent conversations between Krishna, his son Sambo,—who had become, a leper by the curse of Durvasas,—Vasistha, Narada and Vyasa, upon the power and glory of the sun, and the manner in which he is to be worshipped. There is some curious matter in the last chapters, relating to the Magas, silent worshippers of the sun, from Sakadwipa ; as if the compiler had adopted the persian term Magh, and connected the fire worshippers of Iran with those of India. This is a subject, however, that requires further investigation.

The Bhavishyottara is equally with the preceding, a sort of manual of religious offices: the greater portion being appropriated to Vratas, and the remainder, the forms and circumstances with which gifts are to be represented. Many of the ceremonies are obsolete, or are observed in a different manner, as the Rathayatra or car-festival and the Madanotshava or festival of spring. The descriptions of those throw some light upon the public condition of the Hindu religion at a period probably prior to the Mahomedan conquest. The different ceremonies are illustrated by legends, which are, sometimes, ancient; as, for instance, the destruction of the God of love by Siva, and his thence becoming Ananga, the disembodied lord of hearts. The work supposed to be communicated by Krishna to Yudhisthira, at a great assemblage of holy persons at the corronation of the latter, after the conclusion of the great war.

10. Brahma Vaivarta Purana. "That Purana which is related by Savarni to Narada, and contains the account of the greatness of Krishna, with the occurances of the Rathantara where, also, the story of Brahmavaraha is repeatedly told, is called the Brahma Vaivarta, and contains eighteen thousand stanzas." The account here given of the Brahma Vaivarta Purana agrees with its present state, as to its extent. The copies rather exceed than fall short of eighteen thousand stanzrs. It also correctlyrepresents its comprising a Mahatmya or legend of Krishna; but it is very doubtful, nevertheless, if the same work is intended.

The Brahma Vaivárta, as it now exists, is narrated, not by Savarni, but the Rishi Narayana, to Narada, by whom it is communicated to Vyasa;

he teaches it to Suta; and the latter repeats it to the Rishis at Naimisharanya. It is devided into four Khandas or books Brahma, Prakriti, Ganesa, and Krishna Janma Khandas; dedicated severally to describe the acts of Brahma, Devi, Ganesa, and Krishna; the latter, however, throughout absorbing the interest and importance of the work. In none of these is there any account of the Varaha Avatara of Vishnu,—which seems to be intended by Matsya,—nor any reference to a Rathantara Kalpa. It may also be observed, that in describing the merit of presenting a copy of this Purana, the Matsya adds: "whoever makes such gift is honoured in the Brahma-loka;" a sphere which is very inferior in dignity to that to which a worshipper of Krishna is taught to aspire by this Purana. The character of the work is, in truth so decidedly sectarial, and the sect to which it belongs so distinctly marked,—that of the worshippers of the Juvenile Krishna and Radha, a form of belief of known modern origin,—that it can scarcely have found a notice in a work to which, like the Matsya, a much more remote date seems to belong. Although, therefore, the Matsya, may be received in proof of there having been a Brahma Vaivarta Purana at the date of its compilation, dedicated especially to the honour of

Krishna, yet we cannot credit the possibility of its being the same we now possess.

Although some of the legends, believed to be ancient, are scattered through the different portions of this Purana, yet the great mass of it is taken up with tiresome descriptions of Brindavana and Goloka, the dwelling of Krishna on earth and in heaven; endless reqetitions of prayers and invocations addressed to him; and with inspid descriptions of his person and sports, and the love of the Gopis and Radha towards him. There are some particulars of the origin of the artificer-castes,—which are valuable, because it is cited as authority in matters affecting them,—contained in the Brahma Khandas, and in the Prakriti and Ganesa Khandas, are legends of those divinities, not wholly, perhaps modern inventions, but of which the source has not been traced. In the life of Krishna, incidents recorded are the same as those narrated in the Vishnu and in the Bhagavata; but the stories absurd as they are, are much compressed to make room for original matter still more purile and tiresome. The Brahma Vaivarta has not the slightest title to be regarded as a Purana.

11. Linga Purana. Where Maheswara, present in the Agni Linga, explained (the objects of

life) Virtue, Wealth, pleasure and final liberation at the end of the Agni Kalpa, that Purana, consisting of eleven thousand stanzas, was called the Linga by Brahma himself.

The Linga Purana conforms accurately enough to this description. The Kalpa is said to be the Isana, but this is the only difference. It consists of eleven thousand stanzas. It is said to have been originally composed by Brahma; and the primitive Linga is a pillar of radiance, in which Maheswara is present. The work is, therefore, the same as that referred to by the Matsya.

A short account is given in the beginning, of elemental and secondary creation, and of the patriarchal families; in which, however, Siva takes the place of Vishnu, as the indescrible cause of all things. Brief accounts of Siva's incarnations and proceedings in different Kalpas next occur, offering no interest, except as characteristic of sectarial notions. The appearance of the great fiery Linga takes place, in the interval of a creation to separate Vishnu and Brahma, who not only disputes the supremacy, but fights for it; when the Linga snddenly springs up, and puts them both to shame; as after travelling upwards and downwards for a thousand years in each direction, neither can approach to its termination,

Upon the Linga the sacred monosyallable Om is visible; and the Vedas procced from it, by which Brahma and Vishnu become enlightened, and acknowledge and eulogise the superior might and glory of Siva.

A notice of the creation in the Padma Kalpa then follows; and thus leads to praises of Siva and Vishnu and Brahma. Siva repeats the story of his incarnations, twenty-eight in number; intended as a counterpart, no doubt to the twenty-four Avataras of Vishnu, as described in the Bhagabata; and both being amplications of the original ten Avataras, and of much less merit as fictions, Another instance of rivalry occurs in the legend of Dadhichi, a Muni and worshipper of Shiva. In the Bhagavat, there is a strory of Ambarisha being defended against Durvasas by the discus of Vishnu, against which that Saiva sage is helpless. Here Vishnu pulls his discus at Dadhichi: but it falls, blunted, to the ground; and a conflict ensues in which Vishnu and his partisans are all overthrown by the Muni.

A description of the universe, and of the regal dynasties of the Vaivaswata Manwantara to the time of Krishna, runs through a number of chapters in substance, aud very commonly, in words, the same as other Purans; after which the work resumes its proper character narrating legends, and enjoining rites, and reciting prayers intending to do honour to Siva under various forms. Although however, the Linga holds a prominent place amongst them, the spirit of the worship is as little influenced by the character of the type as will be imagined. There is nothing like the phallic orgines of antiquity; it is all mystical and spiritual. The Linga is two-fold, external and internal. The ignorant, who needs a visible sign, worship Siva to a 'mark' or 'type'—which is the proper meaning of the word 'Linga'—of wood or stone: but the wise look upon this outward emblem as nothing, and contemplate, in their minds, the invisible, inscrutable type, which is Siva himself. Whatever may have been the origin of this form of worship in India, the notion upon which it was founded, according to the impure fancies of European writers, are not to be traced in even the Saiva Puranas.

Data for conjecturing the era of this work are defective. But it is more ritual than a Purana; and the Pouranic chapters which it has inserted in order to keep up something of its character, have been, evidently, borrowed for the purpose. The incarnations of Siva, and their 'pupils' as specified in one place, and the importance attached to the practice of the Yoga render it possible that, under the former, are intended those teachers of Ṣaiva religion who belong to the Yoga school, which seems to have flourished about the eighth or ninth century. It is not likely that the work is earlier: it may be considerably later. It has preserved, apparently, some Saiva legends of an early date; but the greater part is ritual and mysticism of comparatively recent introduction.

12. Varaha Purana. "That in which the glory of the great Varaha is predominant, as it was revealed to earth by Vishnu, in connexion, wise Munis, with the Manava Kalpa, aud which contains twenty-four thousand verses, is called the Varaha Purana."

It may be doubted if the Varaha Purana of the present day is here intended. It is narrated by Vishnu and Varaha, or in the boar incarnation to the personified earth. Its extent, however, is not half that specified; little exceeding ten thousand stanzas. It furnishes also itself, evidence of the prior currency of some other work, similarly denominated; as in the description of Mathura contained in it, Sumantu, a Muni, is made to observe, "The divine Varaha in former times expounded a Purana for the purpose of solving the perplexity of Earth."

Nor can Varaha Purana be regarded as a Purana agreeably to the common definition; as it contains but a few scattered and brief allusions to the creation of the world and the reign of kings; It has no detailed geneologies, either of the patriarchal or regal families, and no account of the reigns of the Manus. Like the Linga Purana, it is a religious manual, almost wholly occupied with forms of prayer and rules for devotional observances, addressed to Vishnu; interspered with legendary illustrations, most of which are peculiar to itself, though some are taken from the common and ancient stock. Many of them, rather incompatibly with, the general scope of the compilation, relate to the history of Siva and Durga. A considerable portion of the work is devoted to descriptions of various Tirthas, places of Vaishnava pilgrimage, and one on the Mathura enters into a variety of particulars relating to the shrines of that city constituting the Mathura Mahatmya.

In the sectarianism of the Varaha Purana there is no leaning to the particular adoration of Krishna: nor are the Rathayatra and Janmastomi included amongst the observances enjoined. There are neither indications of its belonging to an earlier stage of Vishnu worship; and it may, perpaps be referred to the age of Ramamya, the early part of the twelfth century.

13. Skanda Purana. "The Skanda Purana, is that in which the six-faced deity (Skanda) has related the events of the Tatpurusha Kalpa, enlarged with many tales, and subservient to the duties taught by Maheswara. It is said to contain eighty-one thousand one hundred stanzas; so it is asserted amongst mankind."

It is uniformly agreed that the Skandha Purana, in a collective form, has no existence; and the fragments in the shape of Samhitas, Khandas, and Mahatmyas, which are affirmed, in various parts of India, to be portions of the Purana, present a much more formidable mass of stanzas than even the immense number of which it is said to consist. The most celebrated of these portions, in Hindustan, is the Kasi Khanda, a very minute description of the temples of Siva in or adjacent to Benares, mixed with directions for worshipping Maheswara, and a great variety of legends explanatory of its merits and of the holiness of Kasi. Many of them are purile and uninteresting; but some are of a higher character. The story of Agastya records, probably, in a legendary style, the propagation of Hinduism in the south of India, and in the history of Divadasa, a king of

Kasi, we have an embellished tradition of the temporary depression of the worship of Siva, even in its metropolis, before the ascendancy of the followers of Buddha; there is every reason to believe the greater part of the contents of the Kasi Khanda anterior to the first attack upon Benares by Mahmud Ghajni. The Kasi Khanda alone contains fifteen thousand stanzas.

Another considerable work ascribed, in Upper India, to a Skanda Purana, is the Utkala Khanda, giving an account of the holiness of Orissa, and the Kshetra of Purushottama or Jagannatha. The same vicinity is the site of temples once of great magnificience and extent, dedicated to Siva, as Bhuvaneshwara, which forms an excuse for attaching an account of a Vaishnava Tirtha to an eminently Saiva Purana. There can be little doubt however, that the Utkala Khanda is unwarrantably included amongst the progeny of the parent work. Besides this, there is a Brahmottara Khanda, a Reva Khanda, a Siva Rahashya Khanda,—a Himavat Khanda and others. Of the Samhitas, the chief are the Suta Samhita, Sanatkumar Samhita, Saura Samhita, and Kapila Samhita, there are several denominated Samhitas. The Mahatmyas are more numerous still. According to the Suta Samhitas as quoted by Colonel Vans Kennedy,

Skanda Puranas contains six Samhitas, five hundred Khandas, and five hundred thousand stanzas; more than what is even attributed to all the Puranas. He thinks judging from internal evidence, that all the Khandas and Samhitas may be admitted to be genuine, though the Mahatmyas have rather questionable appearance. Now one kind of internal evidence is the quantity; and, as no more than eighty-one thouaand one hundred stanzas have ever been claimed for it, all] in excess above that amount must be questionable. But many of the Khandas, the Kasí Khanda for instance, are quite as local, as the Mahatmyas, being legendary stories relating to the erection and sanctity of certain temples, or groups of temples, and to certain Lingas; the interested origin of which renders them, very reasonably, objects of suspicion. In the present state of our acquaintance with the reputed portions of the Skanda Purana, my own view of their authenticity are so opposed to those entertained by Colonel Vans Kennedy, that, instead of admitting all the Samhitas and Khandas to be genuine, I doubt if any one of them was ever a part of the Skanda Purana.

14. Vamana Purana. "That in which the four-faced Brahma taught the three objects of exist

ence, as subservient to the account of the greatness of Trivikrama, which treats, also, of the Siva Kalpa and which consists of ten thousand stanzas, is called the Vamana Purana."

The Vamana Purana contains an account of the dwarf incarnation of Vishnu; but it is related by Pulastya to Narada, and extends to but about seven thousand stanzas. Its contents scarcely establish its claim to the character of a Purana. There is little of order in the subjects which this work recapitulates, and which arise out of replies made by Pulastya to questions put, abruptly and unconnectedly by Narada. The greater part of them relate to the worship of the Linga; a rather strange topic for a Vaishnava Purana, but engrossing the principal part of the compilation. They are, however, subservient to the object of illustrating the sanctity of certain holy places; so that the Vamana Purana is little else than a succession of Mahatmyas. Thus, in the opening, almost, of the work occurs the stoy of Daksha's sacrifice. the object of which is to send Siva to Papamochan Tirtha, at Beneras, where he is released from the sin of Brahmanicide. Next comes the story of burning Kamadeva for the purpose of illustrating the holiness of a Siva Linga at Kedareswara in the Himalaya, and of Badarikasrama.

The larger part of the work consists of the Saro-mahatmya, or legendary examplifications of the holiness of Sthanu Tirtha; that is, of the sanctity of various Lingas and certain Pools at Thansar and Kurukshetra, the country north-west from Delhi. There are some stories, also, relating to the holiness of the Godavary river: but the general site of legends is in Hindustan. In the course of these accounts, we have a long narrative of the marriages of Siva and Uma, and the birth of Karttikeya.

There are a few brief allusions to creation and the Manwantaras; but they are only incidental; and all the five characteristics of a Purana are difficient. In noticing the Swarochisha Manwantara, towards the end of the book, the elevation of Bali-monarch of the Daityas, and his subjugation of the universe, the gods included, are described; and this leads to the narration that gives its little to the Purana, the birth of Krishna as a dwarf for the purpose of humilating Bali by fraud as he was invincible by force. The story is told as usual; but the scene is laid at Kurukshetra.

A more minute examination of this work than that which has been given to it, might perhaps, discover some hint from which to conjecture its date. It is of a more tolerant character than the

Puranas, and divides its homage between Siva and Vishnu with tolerable impartiality. It is not connected, therefore, with any sectarial principles, and may have preceeded their introduction. It has not, however, the air of any antiquity; and its compilation may have assumed the pleasure of some Brahman of Benares three or four centuries ago.

15. Kurma Purana. "That in which Janardan in the form of a tortoise, the regions under the earth, explained the objects of life—duty, wealth, pleasure, and liberation—in communication with Indradyumna and the Rishis in the proximity of Sakra, which refers to the Lakshmi Kalpa, and contains seventeen thousand stanzas, is the Kurma Purana.

In the first chapter of Kurma Purana, It gives an account of itself, which does not exactly agree with his description. Suta who is repeating the narration, is made to say to the Rishis; "This most excellent Kurma Purana is the fifteenth. Samhitas are fourfold, from the variety of the collections. The Brahmi, Bhagavati, Souri, and Vaishnavi are well known as the four Samhitas which confer virtue, wealth, pleasure and liberation. This is the Brahmi Sanhitas, conformable to the four Vedas; in which there are six thousand slokas;

and, by it, the importance of the four objects of life, O great sages, holy knowledge and Parameshwara is known." There is an irreconcilable difference in this specfication of the number of stanzas and that given above. It is not very clear what is meant by a Samhita, as here used.

A Samhita, as observed above, is something different from a Purana. It may be an assemblage of prayers and legends, extracted professedly, from a Purana, but is not, usually, applicable to the original. The four Samhitas here specified refer rather to their religious character than to their connexion with any specific work; and, in fact, the same terms are applied to what are called Samhitas of the Skanda. In this sense, a Purana might be also a Samhita; that is, it might be an assemblage of formulæ and legends belonging to a division of Hindu system; and the work in question, like the Vishnu Purana, does adopt both titles. It says: "This is the excellent Kurma Purna, the fifteenth of the series," and again: "This is the Brahmi Samhita." At any rate, no other work has been met with pretending to be the Kurma Purana.

With regard to the other particulars specified by the Matsya, traces of them are to be found. Although, in two accounts of the traditional communication of the Purana, no mention is made to Vishnu as one of the teachers, yet Suta repeats, at the out set, a dialogue between Vishnu, as the Kurmà and Indradyumna, at the time of the churning of the ocean; and much of the subsequent narrative is put into the mouth of the former.

The name being that of an Avatara of Vishnu, it might lead us to expect a Vaishanava work, but it is always, and correctly, classed with the Saiva Puranas; the greater portion of it inculcating the worship of Siva and Durga. It is divided into two parts, of nearly equal length. In the first part accounts of the creation, of Avataras of Vishnu, of the solar and lunar dynasties of the kings to the time of Krishna, of the universe, and of the Manwantaras, are given, in general in a summary manner, but not unfrequently, in the words employed in the Vishnu Purana. With these are blended hymns addressed to Maheswara by Brahma and others; the defeat of Andhakasura by Bhairava, the origin of four Saktis, Maheswari, Siva, Sati and Haimavati, from Siva; and other Saiva legends. One chapter gives a more distinct and connected account of the incarnations of Siva, in the present age, than the Linga, and it bears, still more, the appearance, of an attempt to identify the teachers of the Yoga school with personations of their preferential deity. Several chapters form Kasi Mahatmya, or legends of Benares. In the second part there are no legends. It is divided into two parts, the Iswara Gita, and Vyasa Gita. In the former, the knowledge of God, that is of Siva, through contemplative devotion, is taught. In the latter the same object is enjoined through works, or observance of the ceremonies and precepts of the Vedas.

The date of the Kurma Purana cannot be very remote; for it is avowedly posterior to the establishment of the Tantrika, the Sakta and the Jaina sects. In the twelfth chapter it is said:—"The Vairava, Vama, Arhata, and Yamala Sastras are intended for delusion. There is no reason to believe that the Vairava and Yamala Tantras are very ancient works, or that the practices of the left hand, Saktas, or the doctrines of Arhat or Jaina, were known in early centuries of our era.

16. Matsya Purana. "That in which for the sake of promulgating the Vedas, Vishnu, in the beginning of a Kalpa related to Manu the story of Narashimha, and the events of several Kalpas; that, O sages, know to be the Matsya Purana, containing twenty thousand stanzas."

We might, it is to be supposed, admit the

description which the Matsya gives of itself to be correct; and yet, as regards the number of verses there seems to be a mis-statement. Three very good copies—one in my possession, one in the Company's library, and one in Radcliffe library—concur in all respects, and in containing no more than between fourteen and fifteen thousand stanzas. In this case Bhagavata is nearer the truth, when it assigns to it fourteen thousand. We may conclude therefore, that the reading of the passage is, in this respect, erroneous. It is correctly said, that the subjects of the Purana were communicated by Vishnu, in the form of fish, to Manu.

The Purana, after the usual prologue of Suta and the Rishis, opens with the accounts of the Matsya or fish Avatara of Vishnu, in which he preserves a king, named Manu, with the seeds of all things, in an ark, from the waters of that inundation which, in the season of a Pralaya, overspreads the world. This story is told in the Mahabharata, with reference to the Matsya as its authority; from which it might be inferred, that the Purana was prior to the poem. This, of course, is consistent with the tradition that the Puranas were first composed by Vyasa. But there can be no doubt that the greater part of the Mahabharata is much older than any extant Purana. The present instance is itself, a proof; for the primitive simplicity with which the story of the fish Avatara is told in the Mahabharata, is of a much more antique complexion than the mysticism and extravagance of the actual Matsya Purana. In the former, Manu collects the seeds of existing things in the ark; it is not said how: in the latter, he brings them together by the power of Yoga. In the latter the great serpent comes to the king, to serve as a cord wherewith to fasten the ark to the horn of the fish: in the former a cable made of ropes is more intelligibly employed for the purpose.

Whilst the ark floats, fastened to the fish, Manu enters into conversation with him; and his questions and the replies of Vishnu form the main substance of the compilation. The first subject is the creation, which is that of Brahma and the patriarchs. Some of the details are the usual ones; others are peculiar, especially those relating to the Pitris or progenitors. The regal dynasties are next described; and then follow chapters on the duties of different orders. It is in relating those of house-holders, in which the duty of making gifts to Brahma is comprehended, that we have the specification of the extent and subjects of the Puranas. It is meritorious to have copies made of them, and to give them away on particular occasions. Thus, it is said, of Matsya: "Whoever gives it away at either equinox, along with a golden fish, and a milch cow, gives away the whole earth," that is he reaps a like reward, in the next migration. Specical duties of the house-holder—Vratas or occa sional acts of piety—are then described at considerable length, with legendary illustrations. The account of the universe is given in the usual strain. Saiva legends ensue; as the destruction of Tripurasura; the war of the gods with Taraka and the Daityas, and the consequent birth of Karttikeya, with the various circumstances of Uma's birth and marriage, the burning of Kamadeva, and other events involved in that nature; the destruction of the Asuras, Maya aud Andhaka; the origin of the Matris, and the like; interspersed with the Vaishnava legends of the Avataras. Some Mahatmyas contain some interesting particulars. There are various chapters on law and morals, and one of which furnishes directions for building houses and making images. We then have an account of the kings of future period; and the Purana concludes with a chapter on gifts.

The Matsya Purana, it will be seen, even from this brief sketch of its contents, is a miscellaneous compilation, but including, in its contents, the elements of a genuine Purana. At the same time it is of too mixed a character to be considered as a genuine work of the Pauranic class; and, upon examining it carefully, it may be suspected that it is indebted to various works, not only for its matter, but for its words. The genealogical and historical chapters are much the same as those of the Vishnu, and many chapters as those on the Pitris and Sraddhas, are precisely the same as those of the Sriti Khanda of the Padma Purana. It has drawn largely also from the Mahabbharata. Amongst other instances, it is sufficient to quote the story of Savitri, the devoted wife of Satyavan, which is given in the Matsya in the same manner, but considerably abridged.

Although a Saiva work, it is not exclusively so; and it has not such sectarial absurdities as the Kurma and Linga. It is a composition of considerable interest; but, if it has extracted its materials from the Padma,—which it also quotes on one occasion, the specification of the Upapuranas,—it is subsequent to that work, and, therefore, not very ancient.

17. Garuda Purana. "That which Vishnu recited in the Garuda Kalpa, relating, chiefly, to the birth of Garuda from Vinata, is here called the Garuda Purana and in it there are read fifteen thousand verses."

The Garuda Purana which has been the subject of my examination corresponds in no respect with this description, and is, probably a different work, though entitled the Garuda Purana. It is identical, however, with two copies in the Company's library. It consists of no more than about seven thousand stanzas; it is repeated by Brahma to Indra; and it contains no account of the birth of Garuda. There is a brief notice of the creation; but the greater part is occupied with description of Vratas or religious observances, of holidays, of sacred places dedicated to the sun, and with prayers from the Tantrika ritual addressed to the sun, to Siva, and to Vishnu. It contains, also, chapters on astrology, palmistry, and precious stones, and one, still more extensive on medicine. The latter portion called the Preta Kalpa, is taken up with directions for the performance of obsequial rites. There is nothing, in all those, to justify the application of the name. Whether a genuine Garuda Purana exists is doubtful. The description given in the Matsya is less particular than even the brief notices of other Puranas and might have easily been written without the knowledge of the book itself; being, with the exception of the number of stanzas, confined to circumstances that the title alone indicates.

18. Brahmanda Purana. "That which has declared, in twelve thousand two hundred verses, the magnificence of the egg of Brahma, and in which the account of the future Kalpa is contained is called the Brahmanda Purana and was revealed by Brahma."

The Brahmanda Purana is usually considered to be in much the same predicament as the Skanda no longer procurable in a collective body, but represented by a variety of Skandas and Mahatmyas, professing to be derived from it. The facility with which any trace may be thus attached to the non-existent original, and the advantage that has been taken of its absence to compile a variety of unauthentic fragments, has given to the Brahmanda, Skanda, and Padma, according to Colonel Wilford, the character, of being "the Puranas of thieves or imposters." This is not applicable to the Padma, which, as above shown, occurs entire and the same in various parts of India. The imposition of which the other two are made the vehicles can deceive no one; as the purpose of the particular legend is always too obvious to leave any doubt of its origin.

Copies of what profess to be the entire Brahmanda Purana are sometimes, though rarely, procurable. I met with one in two portions the former containing one hundred and twenty-four chapters, and the latter, seventy-eight; and the whole containing about the number of stanzas to the Purana. The first and largest portion, however, proved to be the same as the Vayu Purana, with a passage occasionally slightly varied, and at the end of each chapter the common pharse, 'Iti Brahmanda Purane' substituted 'Iti Vayu Purane.' I do not think there was any intended fraud in the substitution. The last section of the first part of Vayu Purana is termed the Brahmanda section, giving an account of the dissolution of the universe and a careless or ignorant transcriber might have taken this for the title of the whole. The checks to the identity of the work have been honestly preserved, both in the index and the frequent specification of Vayu as the teacher or narrator of it. The second portion of this Brahmanda is not any part of the Vayu; it is, probably, current in the Dakhin as a Samhita or Khanda. Agastya is represented as going to the city Kanchi (Conjevram), where Vishnu, as Hayagriva, appears to him, and, in answer to his inquiries, imparts to him the means of salvation, the worship of Parasakti. In illustration of the efficiency of this form of adoration, the main subject of the work is an account of the exploits of the Lalita Devi, a form of Durga and her destruction of the demon Bhandasur. Rules for her worship are decidedly of a Sakta or Tantrika type and his work cannot be admitted, therefore, to be a part of a genuine Purana.

UPAPURANAS.

The Upapuranas, in the few instances which are known, differ a little in extent or subject, from some of those to which the title of Purana is ascribed. The Matsya enumerates but four; but the Devi Bhagavata has a more complete list and specifies eighteen. They are: 1. Sanatkumar, 2. Narasimha, 3. Naradiya, 4. Siva, 5. Durvasasa, 6. Kapila, 7. Manava, 8. Ausanasa, 9. Varuna, 10. Kalika, 11. Samba, 12. Nandi, 13. Saura, 14. Parasara, 15. Aditya, 16. Maheswara, 17. Bhagavata, 18. Vasistha. The Matsya observes, of the second, that is named in the Padma Purana, and contains eighteen thousand verses. The Nandi is called Nanda, and says, that Karttikeya tells, in it, the story of Nanda. A rather different list is given in the Reva Khanda; or: 1. Sanatkumar, 2 Narasimha, 3. Nanda, 4. Sivadharma, 5. Daurvasasa, 6. Bhavishya, related by Narada or Naradiya, 7. Kapila, 8. Manava, 9. Ausanasa, 10. Brahmanda, 11. Varuna, 12. Kalika, 13. Maheswara, 14. Samba 15. Saura, 16. Parasara, 17. Bhagavata, 18. Kaurma. These authorities, however, are of questionable weight; having in view, no doubt, the pretensions of the Devi Bhagavata to be considered as the authentic Bhagavata.

Of these Upapuranas few are to be procured. Those in my possession are the Siva, considered as distinct from the Vayu, the Kalika, and, perhaps one of the Naradiyas, as noticed above. I have, also three of the Skandas of the Devi Bhagavata, which, most undoubtedly, is not the real Bhagavata, supposing that any Purana so named preceded the work of Bopadeva. There can be no doubt that in any authentic list the name of Bhagavata does not occur amongst the Upapuranas: it has been tried there to prove that there are two works so entitled, of which the Purana is the Devi Bhagavata, the Upapurana, the Sri Bhagavata. The true reading should be Bhargava, the Purana of Bhrigu and the Devi Bhagavata is not even an Upapurana. It is very questionable if the entire work, which, as far as it extends, is eminently a Sakta composition, ever had existence.

The Siva Upapurana contains about six thousand stanzas, distributed into two parts. It is related by Sanatkumar to Vyasa and the Rishis at Naimisharanya; and its character may be judged of from the questions to which it is a reply.

"Teach us" said the Rishis, "the rules of worshipping the Linga, and of the god of gods adored under that type: describe to us his various forms, the places sanctified by him, and the prayers with which it is to be addressed." In answer Sanatkumar repeats the Siva Purana, containing the birth of Vishnu and Brahma; the creation and divisions of the universe; the origin of all things from the Linga; the rules of worshipping it and Siva; the sanctity of times, places, and things dedicated to him, the delusion of Brahma and Vishnu by the Linga; rules for various observances in honor of Mahadeva; the mode of practising the Yoga; the glory of Benares and other Siva Tirthas, and the perfection of the objects of life by union with Maheswara. These subjects are illustrated in the first part, with very few legends; but the second is made up almost wholly, of Saiva stories, as the defeat of Tripursura; the sacrifice of Daksha; the births of Karttikeya and Ganesha, (the sons of Siva) and Nandi and Bhringri (his attendants), and others; together with descriptions of Benares and other places of pilgrimage, and rules for observing such festivals as the Sivratri. This work is a Saiva manual, not a Purana.

The Kalika Purana contains about nine thousand stanzas, in ninety-eight chapters, and is only work of the series dedicated to recommend the worship of the bride of Siva, in one or other of her manifold forms, as Girija, Devi, Bhadrakali, Kali, Mahamaya. It belongs, therefore, to the Sakta modification of Hindu belief, or the worship of the female powers of the deties. The influence of this worship shows itself in the very first pages of the work, which relates the incestuous passion of Brahma, for his daughter Sandhya, in a strain that has nothing analogous to it in the Vayu, Linga, or Siva Puranas.

The marriage of Siva and Parvati is a subject early described, with the sacrifice of Daksha, and the death of Sati. And this work is an authority for Siva's carrying the dead body about the world: and the origin of the Pithasthanas or places where the different members of it were scattered, and where Lingas were, consequently, erected. A legend follows of the birth of Bhairava and Vetala whose devotion to different forms of Devi furnishes occasions to describe, in great details, the rites and formulæ of which her worship consists, including the chapters on sanguinary sacrifices, translated in the Asiatic researches. Another pecularity in this work is afforded by very prolix description of a number of rivers and mountains at Kamrupa Tirtha, in Assam, and rendered holy ground by the celebrated temple of Durga in that country, as Kamakshi or Kamaskya. It is a singular, and yet uninvestigated, circumstance, that Assam, or, at least, the north-east of Bengal, seems to have been, in great degree, the source from which the Tantrika and Sakta corruptions of the religion of the Vedas and Puranas proceeded.

The specification of the Upapuranas, whilst it names several of which the existence is problematical, omits other works bearing the same designation, which are sometimes met with. Thus, in the collection of Colonel Mackenzie, we have a portion of the Bhagavata, and a Mudgala Purana, which is, probably the same with the Ganesa Upanishada cited by Colonel Vans Kennedy. I have also, a copy of the Ganesa Upapurana, which seems to agree with that of which he speaks, the second portion being entitled the Krida Khanda, in which the pastimes of Ganesa, including a variety of legendary matters, are described. The main subject of the work is the greatness of Ganesa: and prayers and formulæ appropriate to him are abundantly detailed. It appears to be a work originating with the Ganapatya sect or worshippers of Ganesa. There is, also, a minor Purana called Adi or 'first,' not included in the list. This is a work, however, of no great extent of importance, and is confined to a detail of the sports of the juvenile Krishna. From the sketch thus offered of the subjects of the Puranas, and which, although admitting of collection, is believed to be, in the main, a candid and accurate summary it will be evident, that in their present conditions they must be received with caution, as authorities for the mythological religion of the Hindus at the remote period. They preserve no doubt many ancient notions and traditions; but these have been so much taken up with foreign matter intended to favour the popularity of particular forms of worship, or articles of faith, that they cannot be unreservedly recognized as genuine representations of what we have reason to believe the Puranas originally were.

The safest sources, for the ancient legends of the Hindus, after the Vedas, are no doubt, the two great poems, the Ramayana and Mahabharata. The first offers only a few; but they are of a primitive character. The Mahabharata is more fertile in fiction; but it is more miscellaneous; and much that it contains is of equivocal authenticity and uncertain date. Still, it affords many materials that are genuine: and it is, evidently, the great fountain from which most, if not all, of the Puranas have drawn; as it intimates, itself, when it declares, that there is no legend current in the world which has not its origin in the mahabharata.

A work of some extent, professing to be part of the Mahabharata, may, more accurately, be ranked with the Pauranik compilations of least authenticity and latest origin. The Harivamsa is chiefly occupied with the adventures of Krishna; but, as introductory to his era, it records particulars of the creation of the world, and of the patriarchal and regal dynasties. This is done with much carelessness and inaccurancy of compilation; as I have had occasion, frequently, to notice in the following pages. The work has been very industriously translated by M. Langlois.

AN ACCOUNT OF VISHNUPURAN.

A comparism of the subjects of the following pages with those of the other Puranas will sufficiently show, that, of the whole series, the Vishnu most closely conforms to the definition of a Pancha Lakshana Purana, or one which treats of five specified topics. It comprehends them all; and although it has infused a portion of extraneous and sectarial matter, it has done so with sobriety and with judgement, and has not suffered the fervour of its religious zeal to transport it into very wide deviations from the prescribed path. The legendary tales which it has inserted are few, and are conveniently arranged, as that they do not distract the attention of the compiler from objects of more permanent interest and importance.'

The first book of the six, into which the work is divided, is occupied chiefly with the details of creation, primary (Sarga) and secondary (Pratisarga); the first explaining how the universal proceeds from Prakriti or eternal crude matter; the second in what manner the forms of things are developed from the elementary substances previously evolved, or how they reappear after their temporary destruction. Both these creations are periodical; but the termination of the first occurs only at the end of the life of Brahma, when not only all the gods and all other forms are annihilated, but the elements are again merged into primary substances, besides which, one only spiritual being exists. The latter takes place at the end of every Kalpa or day of Brahma, and affects only the forms of inferior creatures, and lower world; leaving the substance of the universe entire, and sages and gods unharmed. The explanation of these events involves a description of the periods of time upon which they depend, and which are, accordingly, detailed. Their character has been a source of every unnecessary perplexity to European writers; as they belong to a scheme of chronology wholly mythological, having no reference to any real or supposed history of the Hindus, applicable, according to their system, to the infinite and eternal revolutions of the universe. In those notions, and in that of the co-eternity of the spirit and matter, the theogony and cosmogouy of the Puranas, as they appear in the Vishnu Purana, belong to and illustrate systems of high antiquity, of which we have only fragmentary traces in the records of their nations.

The course of the elemental creation is, in the Vishnu, as in other Puranas, taken from the Sankya philosophy; but the agency that operates upon passive matter is confusedly exhibited, in consequence of a partial adoption of the illusory theory of the Vedanta philosophy, and the prevalence of Pauranik doctrine of pantheism. However incompatible with the independent existence of Pradhan or crude matter, and however, incongrous with the separate condition of pure spirit or Purusha, it is declared, repeatedly, that Vishnu, as one with the Supreme Being, is not only spirit, but crude matter and not only the latter, but all visible substance and Time. He is a Purusha, 'spirit'; Pradhana, 'curde matter'; Vyakta, 'visible form' and

Kala, 'time.' This cannot but be regarded as a departure from the primitive dogmas of the Hindus in which the distinctness of the Deity and his works was enunciated; in which, upon his willing the world to be, it was; and in which his interposition in creation, held to be inconsistent with the quiescene of perfection, was explained away by the personification of attributes in action, which afterwards came to be considered as real divinities, Brahma, Vishnu, and Siva, charged severally, for a given season, with the creation, preservation and temporary annahilation of material forms. These divinities are, in the following pages, consistently with the tendency of a Vaishnava work, declared to be no other than Vishnu. In Saiva Puranas, they are in like manner, identified with Siva; the Puranas thus displaying and explaining incompatibility, of which there are traces in other ancient mythologies, between three distinct hypostases of one superior deity, and the indentification of one other of those hypostases with their common and separate original.

After the world has been fitted for the reception of living creatures, it is peopled by the will-engendered sons of Brahma, the Prajapatis or patriarchs, and their posterity. It would seem as if a primitive tradition of the descent of mankind from seven holy personages had at first prevailed, but that, in the course of time, it had been expanded into complicated, and not always consistent, amplification. How could these Riahis or patriarchs have posterity? It was necessary to provide them with wives. In order to account for their existence, the Manu Swayambhuva and his wife Satarupa were added to the scheme. Or Brahma became twofold, male and female; and daughters are then begotten, who are married to the Prajapatis. Upon this basis various legends of Brahma's double nature, some, no doubt, as old as the Vedas, have been constructed. But, although they may have been derived, in some degree, from the authentic tradition of the origin of mankfnd from a single pair, yet the circumstances intended to give more interest and precision to the story are, evidently, of an allegorical or mystical description, and conducted, in apparently later times, to a course of realization which was neither the letter nor spirit of the original legend. Swayambhuva, the son of the self-born or uncreated, and his wife Satarupa, the hundred-formed or multiform, are, themselves, allegories; and their female descendants, who became the wives of the Rishis, are Faith, Devotion, Content, Intelligence, Tradition, and the like; whilst, amongst their posterity, we have the different phases of the moon and the sacrificial fires. In another creation, the chief source of creatures is the patriarch Daksha (ability), whose daughters—virtues, or Passions, or Astronomical Phenomena—are the mothers of all existing things. These legends, perplexed as they appear to be, seem to admit of allowable selection, in the conjecture that the Prajapatis and Rishis were real personages, the authors of the Hindu system of social, moral, and religious obligations, and the first observers of the heavens, and teachers of astronomical science.

The regal personages of Swayambhuva Manwantara are but few; but they are described, in the outset, as governing the earth in the dawn of society and as introducing agriculture and civilization. How much of their story rests upon a traditional remembrance of their actions, it would be useless to conjecture; although there is no extravagance in supposing that the legends relate to a period prior to full establishment, in India, of the Brahmanical institutions. The legends of Dhruva and Prahlada, which are intermingled with these particulars, are, in all probability, ancient; but they are amplified, in a strain conformable to the Vaishnava purport of this Purana, by doctrines and prayers asserting the identity of Vishnu with Supreme. It is clear that the stories do not originate with this Purana. In that of Pralhada, particularly, as hereafter pointed out circumstances essential to the completeness of the story are only alluded to, not recounted; showing, indisputably, the writer having availed himself of some prior authority for his narration.

The second book opens with a continuation of the kings of the first Manwantara; amongst whom, Bharata is said to have given a name to India, called after him, Bharata-Varsha. This leads to a detail of the geographical system of the Puranas, with mount Meru, the seven circular continents, and their surrounding oceans, to the limits[1] of the world; all of which are mythological fiictiôns, in which there is little reason to imagine that any topographical truths are concealed. With regard to Bharata or India, the case is different. The mountains and rivers which are named are readily verifiable; and the cities and the nation, that are particularized may, also in many instances, be proved to have had a real existence. The list is not a very long one, in the Vishnu Purana, and is probably, abridged from some more ample detail, like that which the Mahabharata affords, and which in the hope of supplying information with respect to a subject yet imperfectly investigated, the ancient political condition of India, I have inserted and calculated.

The description which this book also contains of the planetary and other spheres, is equally mythological, although occasionally presenting practical details and motion in which there is an approach to accuracy. The concluding legend of Bharata—in his former life, the king so named, but now a Brahman, who acquires true wisdom, and thereby attains, liberation—is, palpably, an invention of the compiler and is peculiar to this Purana.

The arrangement of the Vedas aud other writings considered sacred by the Hindus—being in fact, the authorities of their religious rites and belief,—which is described in the beginning of the third book, is of much importance to the history of Hindu literature and of the Hindu religion. The sage Vyasa is here represented, not as the author but the arranger or compiler, of the Vedas, the Itihasas, and Puranas. His name denotes his character, meaning the 'arranger' or 'distributor;' and the recurrence of many Vyasas, many individuals who re-modelled the Hindu scriptures, has nothing, in it, that is improbable, except the fabulous intervals by which their labors are separated. The re-arranging, the re-fashioning, of old materials is nothing more than the progress of time would be likely to render necessary. The last recognizing compilation is that of Krishna

Dwaipayana, assisted by Brahmans, who were already conversant with the subjects respectively, assigned to them. They were the members of the College, or school, supposed by the Hindus to have flourished in a period more remote, no doubt, than the truth, but not at all unlikely to have been instituted at some time prior to the accounts of India which we owe to Greek writers and in which we see, enough of the system to justify our inferring that it was then entire. That there have been other Vyasas and other schools since that date, that Brahmins unknown to fame have remodelled some of the Hindu scriptures, and especially the Puranas, cannot reasonably be contested, after dispassionately weighing the strong internal evidence, which all of them afford, of their intermixture of unauthorised and comparatively modern ingredients. But the same internal testimony furnishes proof equally decisive, of the anterior existence of ancient materials; and it is therefore, as idle as it is irrational, to dispute the antiquity or authenticity of the greater portion of the contents of the Puranas, in the face of abundant positive and circumstantial evidence of the prevalence of the doctrines which they teach, the currency of the legends which they narrate, and the integrity of the institutions which they describe at least three centuries before the Christian era. But the origin and development of their doctrines, traditions, and institutions were not the work of a day; and the testimony that establishes their existence three centuries before Christianity, carries it back to a much more remote antiquity, to an antiquity that is, probably, not surpassed by any of the prevailing fictions, institutions, or beliefs of the ancient world.

The remainder of the third book describes the leading institutions of the Hindus, the duties of caste, the obligations of different stages of life, and the celebration of obsequial rites, in a short but primitive strain, and in harmony with the laws of Manu. It is a distinguishing feature of the Vishnu Purana, and it is characteristic of its being the work of no earlier period than most of the Puranas, that it enjoins no sectarial or other acts of supererogation; no Vratas, or occasional self imposed observances, no holiday, no birthdays of Krishna, no nights dedicated to Lakshmi; no sacrifices or modes of worship other than those conformable to the ritual ot the Vedas. It contains no Mahatmys or golden legends, even of the temples in which Vishnu is adored.

The fourth book contains all that the Hindus

have of their ancient history. It is a tolerably comprehensive list of dynasties and individuals; it is a barren record of events. It can scarcely be doubted, however, that much of it is a genuine chronicle of persons, if not of occurances. That it is discredited by palpable absurdities in regard to the longevity of the princes of the earlier dynasties, must be granted; and the particulars preserved of some of them, are trival and fabulous. Still, there is an artificial simplicity and consistency in the succession of persons, and a possibility and probability in some of the transactions, which give to these traditions the semblance of authenticity, and render it likely, that these are not altogether without foundation. At any rate, in the absence of all other sources of information, the record, such as it is, deserves not to be altogether set aside. It is not essential to its celebrity, or its usefulness, that any exact chronological adjustment of the different reigns should be attempted. Their distribution amongst the several Yugas, undertaken by Sir William Jones, or his Pandits, finds no countenance from the original texts, further than an identical notice of the age in which a particular monarch ruled, or the general fact that the dynasties prior to Krishna precede the time of the great war and the beginning of the Kali age, both [which events are placed five thousand years ago. To that age the solar dynasty of princes offers ninety-three descents, the lunar, but forty-five; though they both commence at the same time. Some names may have been added to the former list, some omitted in the latter; and it seems most likely, that notwithstanding their synchronous beginning, the princes of the lunar race were subsequent to those of the solar dynasty. They avowedly branched off from the solar line; and the legend of Sudyumna that explains the connexion, has every appearance of having been contrived for the purpose of referring it to a period more remote than the truth. Deducting, however, from the larger number of princes a considerable proportion, there is nothing to shock probability in supporting, that the Hindu dynasties and their ramifications were spread through an interval of about twelve centuries anterior to the war of the Mahabharata, and, conjecturiug that event to have happened about fourteen centuries before Christianity thus carrying the commencemen: of the legal dynasties of India to about two thousand six hundred years before that date. This, may, or may not, be too remote; but it is sufficient, in a subject where precision is impossibie, to be satisfied with the general impression, that, in the dynasties of kings detailed in the Puranas, we have a record which, although it can not fail to have suffered detriment from age, and may have been injured by careless or injudicious compilation, preserves an account not wholly undeserving of confidence, of the establishment and succession of regular monarchies, amongst the Hindus, from as early an era, and for as continuous a duration, as any in the credible annals of mankind.

The circumstances that are told of the first princes have evident relation to the colonization of India, and the gradual extension of the authority of new races over an uninhabitant or uncivilized region. It is commonly admitted, that the Brahmanical religion and civilization were brought into India from without. Certainly there are tribes on the borders, and in the heart of the country, who are still not Hindus, and passages in the Ramayana and Mahabharata, and Manu, and the uniform tradition of the people themselves, point to a period when Bengal, Orrissa, and the whole of the Dakhin were inhabited by degraded or out-caste, that is, by barbarous, tribes. The traditions of the Puranas confirm these views; but they lend no assistance to the determination of the question whence the Hindus came; whether from a central asiatic nation, as Sir William Jones supposed, or from the Caucasian mountain, the plains of Babyonia, or the borders of the Caspian, as conjectured by Klaproth, Vans Kennedy, and Schlegel. The affinities of Sankrit language prove a common origin of the new widely scattered nations amongst whose dialects they are traceable, and render it unquestionable that they must all have spread abroad from some central spot in the part of the globe first inhabited by mankind, according to the inspired record. Whether any indication of such an event be discoverable in the Vedas, remains to be determined; but it would have been obviously incompatible with the Pauranik system to have referred the origin of Indian princes and principalities to other than native sources. We need not, therefore, expect from them any information as to the foreign derivation of the Hindus.

We have, then, wholly insufficient means for arriving at any information concerning the Anti-Indian period of Hindu History beyond the general conclusion derivable from the actual presence of barbarous and, apparently, aboriginal tribes—from the admitted progressive extension of Hinduism into parts of India, where it did not prevail when the code of Manu was compiled—from the general use of dialects in India, more or less copious, which are different from Sanskrit—and from the affinities of that language with forms of speech current in the western world—that a people who spoke Sanskrit, and followed the religion of the Vedas, came into India, in some very distant age, from land west of the Indus. Whether the date and circumstances of their immigratien will ever be ascertained, is extremely doubtful : but it is difficult to form a plausible outline of their early site and progressive colonization.

The earliest seat of the Hindus, within the confines of Hindustan, was, undoubtedly, the eastern confines of the Panjab. The holy land of Manu and the Puranas lies between the Drishadwati and Sataswati rivers,—the Caggar and Sursooty of our barbarous maps. Various adventures of the first princes and most famous sages occur in this vicinity; and the Asrams or religious domiciles or several of the latter are placed on the bank of the Saraswati. According to some authorities, it was the abode of Vyasa, the compiler of the Vedas and Purans; and, agreeably to another, when, on one occasion, the Vedas had fallen into disuse and been forgotten, the Brahmanas were instructed in them by Saraswata, the son of Saraswti. One of the most distinguished of the tribes of the Brahmanas is known as the Saraswata; and the same word was employed, by Mr. Colebrooke, to denote that modification of Sanskrit which is termed generally Prakriti, and which, in this case, he supposes to have been the language of the Saraswata nation, "which occupied the banks of the river Saraswati." The river itself receives its appelleation from Saraswati, the goddess of learning, under whose auspicies the sacred literature of the Hindus assumed shape and authority. These indications render it certain, that, whatever creeds were imported from without, it was in the country adjacent to the Saraswati river that they were first planted, and cultivated, and reared in Hindusthan.

The tract of land thus assigned for the first establishment of Hinduism in India, is of very circumscribed extent, and could not have been the site of any numerous tribe or nation. The traditions that evidence the early settlement of the Hindus in this quarter, ascribe to the settlers more of a philosophical and religious, than of a seculior character, and combine, with the very narrow bounds of the holy land, to render it possible, that the earliest emigrants were the members, not of a political, so much as of a religious community; that they were a colony of priests, not in the restricted sense in which we use the term, but in that in which it still applies in India, to an Agrahara, a village or hamlet of Brahmans who, although married, and having families, and engaging in tillage, in domestic duties, and in the conduct of secular interests affecting the community, are still supposed to devote their principal attention to sacred study and religious offices. A society of this description, with its artificers and servants, and, perhaps, with a body of martial followers, might have found a home in the Brahmanvarta of Manu, the land, which thence, was entitled the 'holy,' or more literally, "the Brahman, religious," and may have communicated to the rude, uncivilized, unlettered aborigines, the rudiments of social organization, literature, and religion; and partly, in all probability, brough along with them, and partly devised and fashioned by degrees, for the growing necessities of new conditions of society. Those, with whom this civilization commenced, would have had ample inducements to prosecute their successful work; and in the course of time, the improvement, which germinated on the banks ef the Saraswati, was extended beyond the borders of the Jumna and the Ganges.

We have no satisfactory intimation of the stages by which the political organization of the people of Upper India traversed the space between the Saraswati and the more easterly country, where it seems to have taken a concentrated form, and whence it diverged, in various directions, throughout Hindustan. The Manu of the period, Vaivaswata, the son of the sun, is regarded as the founder of Ayodhya; and that city contained to be the capital of the most celebrated branch of his descendants, the posterity of Ikshwaku. The Vishnu Purana evidently intends to describe the tradition of conquest or colonization from this spot, in the accounts it gives of the dispersion of Vaivaswata's prosperity; and although it is difficult to understand what could have led early settlers in India to such a site, it is not inconveniently situated as a commanding position whence emigrations might proceed to the east, the west, and the south. This seems to have happened. A branch from the house of Ikshwaku spread into Tirhoot constituting the Maithili kings and the posterity of another of Vaivaswata's sons reigned at Vaisati, in Southern Tirhoot, or Sarun.

The most adventurous emigration, however, took place through the lunar dynasty, which as observed above, originates from the solar; making in fact, but one race and source for the whole. Leaving out of consideration the legend of

Sudyumna's double transformations, the first prince of Pratishthana, a city south from Ayodhya, was one of Vaivaswata's children, equally with Ikshwaku. The sons of Pururavas, the second of this branch extended by themselves, or their posterity, in every direction: to the east, to Kasi, Magadha, Benares, and Behar; southwards, to the Vindhya hills, and across them, to Vidharva or Behar; and westward along the Narmada, to Kusasthali or Dwarka, in Gujrat; and in a northwesterly direction to Mathura and Hastinapur. These movements are very distinctly discoverable amidst the circumstances narrated in the fourth book of the Vishnu Purana, and are precisely such as might be expected from a radiation of colonies from Ayodhya. Intimations also occur of settlements in Bengal, Kalinga, and the Dakshin; but they are brief and indistinct, and have the appearance of additions subsequent to the comprehension of those countries within the pale of Hindustan.

Besides these traces of migration and settlement, several curious circumstances, not likely to be unauthorized inventions, are hinted in these historical traditions. The distinction of castes was not fully developed prior to the colonization. Of the sons of Vaivaswata, some, as kings were Kshatriyas; but one founded a tribe of Brahmans and another became a Vaisya, and a fourth, a Sudra. It is also said, of other princes, that they established the four castes amongst their subjects. There are also various notices of Brahmanical Gotras or families proceeding from Kshatriya races and there are several indications of severe struggles between the two ruling castes, not for temporal but for spiritual dominion—the right to teach the Vedas. This seems to be the especial purport of the inveterate hostility that prevailed between the Brahmana Vasistha, and Kshatriya Viswamitra, who, as the Ramayan relates, compelled the gods to make him Brahmana also, and whose posterity became celebrated as the Kausika Brahmana. Other legends, again such as Daksha's sacrifice, denote sectarian strife; and the legend of Parasurama reveals a conflict even for temporal authorities, between the two ruling castes. More or less weight will be attached to these conjectures, according to the temperament of different inquirers. But, even, whilst fully aware of the facility with which plausible deductions may cheat the fancy, and little disposed to relax all curb upon the imagination, I find it difficult to regard these legends as wholly unsubstantial fictions, or devoid of all resemblance to the realities of the past.

After the date of the great war, the Vishnu

Purana, in common with those Puranas, which contain similar lists, specifies kings, and dynasties with greater precision, and offers political and chronological particulars to which, on the score of probability, there is nothing to object. In truth their general accuracy has been incontrovertibly established. Inscriptions on columns of stone, on rocks, on coins, deciphered only of late years, through the extraordinary ingenuity and perseverance of Mr, James Prinsep, have verified the names of races and titles of princes—the Gupta and Andhra Rajas, mentioned in the Puranas—and have placed beyond dispute the identity of Chadragupta and Sandrocoptus; thus giving us a fixed point from which to compute the date of other persons and events. Thus the Vishnu Puran specifies the interval, between the Chandragupta and the great war, to be eleven hundred years; and the occurance of the latter little more than fourteen centuries B. C. as shown in my observations on the passage, remarkably concurs with inferences of the like date from different premises. The historical notices that then follow are considerably confused; but they probably afford an accurate picture of the political distraction of India at the time when they were written, and much of the perplexity arises from the corrupt state of the manu cripts, the obscure brevity of the record, and our total want of the means of collateral illustration.

The fifth book of the Vishnu Purana is exclusively occupied with the life of Krishna. This is one of the distinguishing characteristics of the Purana, and is one argument against its antiquity. It is possible, though not yet proved, that Krishna as an Avatara of Vishnu, is mentioned in an indisputably genuine text of the Vedas. He is conspicuously prominent in the Mahabharata, but very contradictorily described there. The part that he usually performs is that of a mere mortal; although the passages are numerous that attach divinity to his person. There are, however, no descriptions, in the Mahabharata, of his juvenile frolics, of his sports in Brindabana, his pastimes with the cow-boys, or even his destruction of the Asuras sent to kill him. These stories have, all, a modern complexion; they do not harmonize with the ancient legend, which, is generally, grave, and, sometimes, majestic. They are the creation of a purile taste and grovelling imagination. These chapters of the Vishnu Purana offer some difficulties as to their originality. They are the same as those on the same subject in the Brahma Purana; they are not very dissimilar to those of the Bhagavata. The latter has some incidents which the

Vishnu has not, and may, therefore, be thought to have improved upon the prior narrative of the latter. On the other hand, abridgement is equally a proof of posterity, as amplification, The simpler style of Vishnu Purana is, however, in favour of its priority; and miscellaneons composition of the Brahma Purana renders it likely to have borrowed these chapters from the Vishnu. The life of Krishna in the Hari Vamsha and the Brahma Vaivarta are, indisputably, of later origin.

The last contains an account of the dissolution of the world, in both its major and minor cataclysms; and, in the particulars of the end of all things by fire and water, as well as in the principle of their perpetual renovation, presents a faithful exhibition of opinions that were general in the ancient world. The metaphysical annihilation of the universe, by the release of the spirit from bodily existence, offers, as already remarked, other analogies to doctrines and practices taught by Pythagoras and Plato, and by the Platonic Christians of later days.

The Vishnu Purana has kept very clear of particulars from which an approximation to its date may be conjectured. No place is described of which the sacredness has any known limit, nor any work cited of probable recent composition.

The Vedas, the Purana, other works forming the body of Sanskrit literature, are named ; and so is the Mahabharata, to which, therefore, it is subsequent. Both Buddhas and Jainas are adverted to. It was, therefore, written before the former had dissappeared. But they existed, in some parts of India, as late as the twelfth century, at least; and it is probable that the Puranas were compiled before that period. The Gupta kings reigned in the seventh century. The historical record, of the Puranas which mentions them, was therefore, later : and there seems little doubt that the same alludes to the first incursions of the Mahomedans, which took place in the eighth century, which brings it still lower. In describing the later dynasties, some, if not all, of which were, no doubt, contemporary, they are described as reigning, altogether, one thousand seven hundred and ninety-six years. Why this duration should have been chosen does not appear ; unless, in conjunction with the number of years which are said to have elapsed between the Great War and the last of the Andhra dynasty which preceded these different races, and which amounted to two thousand three hundred and fifty, the compiler was influenced by the actual date at which he wrote. The aggregate of the two periods would be the Kali year 4149, equivalent to A. D. 1045.

There are some variety and indistinctness in the enumeration of the periods which compose this total: but the date which results it is not unlikely to be an approximation to that of the Vishnu Purana.

It is the boast of inductive philosophy, that it draws its conclusions from the careful observation and accumulation of facts; and it is, equally, the business of all philosophical research to determine its facts before it ventures upon speculation. This procedure has not been observed in the investigation of mythology and traditions of the Hindus. Impatience to generalize has availed itself greedily of whatever promised to afford materials for generalization; and the most erroneous views have been confidently advocated, because the guides to which their authors trusted were ignorant or insufficient. The information gleaned by Sir William Jones was rather in an early season of Sanskrit study, before the field was cultivated. The same may be said of the writings of Paslinoda S. Bartolomeo, with the further disadvantage of his having been imperfectly acquainted with the Sanskrit language and literature, and his veiling his dificiencies under loftiness of pretension and a prodigal display of misapplied erudition. The documents, to which Wilford trusted, proved to be, in great part, fabrications, and where genuine were mixed up with so much loose and unauthenticated matter and so overwhelmed with extravagance of speculation, that his citations need to be carefully and skilfully sifted, before they can be serviceably employed. The descriptions of Ward are too deeply tinctured by his prejudices to be implicity confided in; and they are also derived, in a great measure, from the oral or written communications of some Pandits, who are not, in general, very deeply read in the authorities of their mythology. The accounts of Polier were, in like manner, collected from questionable sources; and his Mythologie des Indous presents an heterogeneous mixture of popular and Puranik tales, of ancient traditions, and legends apparently invented for the occasion, which renders the publication worse than useless, except in the hands of those who can distinguish the pure metal from the alloy. Such are the authorities to which Maurice, Taber, and Crenzer have exclusively trusted, in their description of the Hindu mythology; and it is no marvel that there should have been an utter confounding of good and bad in their selection of materials, and an inextricable mixture of truth and error in their conclusions.

—:o:—